New Almond Cookery

By

Michelle Schmidt

Simon and Schuster
New York

Copyright © 1984 by the California Almond Growers Exchange
All rights reserved
including the right of reproduction
in whole or in part in any form
Published by Simon and Schuster
A Division of Simon & Schuster, Inc.
Simon & Schuster Building
Rockefeller Center
1230 Avenue of the Americas
New York, New York 10020
SIMON AND SCHUSTER and colophon are registered
trademarks of Simon & Schuster, Inc.
Designed by Busse & Cummins, Inc.
Manufactured in the United States of America
Printed by R. R. Donnelley & Sons Co.
Bound by R. R. Donnelley & Sons Co.
1 2 3 4 5 6 7 8 9 10
Library of Congress Cataloging in Publication Data

Schmidt, Michelle.
New almond cookery.
Includes index.
1. Cookery (Almonds) I. Title.
TX814.2.A44S36   1984   641.6'455   84-10634
ISBN: 0-671-52490-9

CONTENTS

ABOUT THE AUTHOR

"A recipe is rather like a marriage – a wedding of flavors, textures and colors," says Michelle Schmidt.

Michelle's skill at marrying flavors and foods received an early lift during years in France (including wine seminars at Stephen Spurrier's Académie). But her deepest roots are in the new California cookery, which emphasizes fresh, fresh ingredients prepared with a high regard for natural flavor and stylish presentation.

Michelle graduated from the California Culinary Academy in San Francisco and later taught there. An English literature major at the University of Virginia, she has recently been writing about food for national magazines. Her recipe comments sound so delicious they are almost fattening.

The author lives on San Francisco's famous Telegraph Hill, just a few hours from the almond orchards where the nuts that inspired this cookbook are harvested.

To Michelle, a perfect meal begins and ends with almonds. A few almonds with sherry for an appetizer...and a glorious chocolate almond torte for dessert. Accused of being single-minded about almonds, she agrees she is a little "nutty" on the subject. "But after all," she says, "madness is only a state of mind."

NOTES TO THE COOK

Robert Farrar Capon
Food for Thought

Recipes are written after the fact. They are mere—and approximate—records, in an alien medium, of glories that exist properly only in the cooking and the eating of good food. They are to cookery what notation is to music: written suggestions from one artist to another.

It is always with some trepidation that one sends recipes out into the world. Cooking is an interpretive art and, as one of the chefs I trained under used to say, relies on a series of happy accidents. This is not to take away from the skill and training of the cook but to recognize the infinite variables one may encounter.

Buddhists say that one never steps into the same river twice. In the culinary sense, one never slices the same lemon twice or grills the same steak. The juice of this lemon may be more acidic than the one used yesterday, requiring a restrained hand as the cook adds drops to finish a sauce. Today's steak, the same cut as last week's, may be leaner, necessitating a soak in a marinade to approximate the tender, juicy glory of the former. The answer is to examine, to touch, to smell, to taste – always assessing and adjusting. After the equipment, the books, and the classes, a skilled technician is transformed into a fine cook by relying on the senses.

On a practical level, buy the best ingredients possible and treat them with respect. Make only thoughtful and informed substitutions. Read the recipe through completely, cooking mentally as you go. Do all the peeling, dicing, and the like before beginning to cook, so that work flows smoothly once you start. Grease pans and heat ovens in advance. Cook food until it is done to your liking; times are approximate and may vary from pan to pan or oven to oven. And then relax.

To prepare and break bread with friends and loved ones is a daily blessing, worthy of joy and meditation.

ALMOND APPLE CURRY SOUP

Soup is such a civilized way to begin a meal. It slows the pace and gently introduces the diner to the delights to come. This curry-scented soup combines the rich, nutty flavor of almond butter with the tart fruitiness of apple. It is a fine beginning to a festive meal.

1 onion, chopped

1 green apple, peeled and diced

¼ cup butter

2 cloves garlic, chopped finely

1 tablespoon curry powder

½ teaspoon salt

2½ cups chicken stock

½ cup almond butter (see On Almonds)

1½ teaspoons lemon juice

Sauté onion and apple in butter until soft. Add garlic, curry powder, and salt. Cook 2 to 3 minutes longer. Add chicken stock and simmer 15 minutes. Purée, in batches, adding almond butter to last batch. Heat through; *do not boil.* Stir in lemon juice. 4 servings.

FIGS WITH LIME AND PEPPER

In a world of immediate everything, a perfectly ripe fig becomes even more delightful because one must wait for fresh figs. The short season invites a mild form of gluttony that manifests itself in the frequent serving of figs — figs alone, figs with prosciutto, figs with cream, and here, figs with almonds, lime, and black pepper.

¼ cup chopped, natural almonds
Pinch salt
1 teaspoon butter
4 large, fresh figs

½ lime, juiced
¼ teaspoon freshly ground, black pepper
Lime slices for garnish

Sauté almonds in salt and butter; cool. Meanwhile, quarter figs and arrange on a serving plate. Drizzle with lime juice and sprinkle with pepper and toasted almonds. Garnish with lime slices.

4 servings.

MELON WITH BASIL AND GINGER

Beginning a meal with sweet, ripe melon is often the perfect choice — especially for weary palates and waning appetites. Here the flavors of ginger, lime, basil, and buttered, toasted almonds are a lively combination.

3 tablespoons chopped, natural almonds

1 teaspoon butter

¼ cup lime juice

1½ teaspoons finely chopped, fresh basil or ½ teaspoon dried basil

1½ teaspoons finely chopped, crystallized ginger

½ cantaloupe, peeled, seeded, and sliced

Sauté almonds in butter until crisp; reserve. Combine lime juice, basil, and ginger. Arrange melon on serving plate. Sprinkle with almonds and drizzle with dressing.

4 servings.

CURRIED EGG SALAD

Most people are indifferent to egg salad. It brings back memories of childhood lunches or suggests a sandwich at the desk on crazy days at the office. This adult version has the intriguing flavors of curry spices and lime juice. A good beginning for a light meal or fine with tea. By substituting 8 slices of pumpernickel for the dainty toast points and adding some sliced tomato, one can end up with four serious sandwiches.

½ cup chopped, natural almonds
1 tablespoon olive oil
½ cup mayonnaise
2 shallots, finely chopped
1 tablespoon lime juice
1½ teaspoons curry powder
1 teaspoon ground cumin
½ teaspoon salt
Pinch cayenne
6 hard-cooked eggs, chopped
6 slices white bread, crusts trimmed, toasted, and cut in half diagonally
2 tablespoons chopped, fresh parsley

Sauté almonds in oil until crisp; cool. Mix almonds with next seven ingredients; fold in chopped eggs. Divide mixture among toast triangles. Sprinkle with parsley. 6 servings.

TUNA WITH CAPERS, RAISINS, AND TOMATO

This luscious tuna salad, in the Italian style, is full of sophisticated flavors. Its heart lies in imported tuna packed in olive oil. One could substitute drained, water-packed tuna and add additional oil, but the dish would lose a bit of character. Served on individual plates accompanied by a few toasted, thin slices of French bread, it is a piquant first course. The buffet table, cocktail hour, or midnight sandwich construction are equally appropriate occasions.

1 tablespoon lemon juice

1 tablespoon tomato paste

¾ teaspoon chopped, fresh marjoram or ¼ teaspoon dried marjoram

¼ teaspoon salt

½ teaspoon freshly ground, black pepper

¼ cup olive oil

7 ounces Italian tuna packed in olive oil, undrained

¼ cup raisins, soaked in boiling water for 20 minutes and drained

½ cup blanched, slivered almonds, toasted

¼ cup thinly sliced scallions

2 tablespoons capers

Combine first five ingredients. Gradually beat in oil. Toss with remaining ingredients. Take care not to overmix.

6 servings.

STUFFED ARTICHOKES

4 medium, fresh artichokes
2 tablespoons lemon juice, divided
¾ cup whole, natural almonds, toasted
¾ cup fresh, white bread crumbs
¾ cup freshly grated, Parmesan cheese
½ cup chopped, fresh parsley
¼ cup butter, softened
2 tablespoons chopped shallots

1 teaspoon grated lemon peel
2 cloves garlic, chopped finely
9 tablespoons olive oil, divided
½ cup water
½ teaspoon salt
¼ teaspoon freshly ground, black pepper

Trim stem, remove tough outer leaves, and slice ⅓ off the top of each artichoke. Gently spread the leaves apart and remove the choke (thistle portion) from the center with a metal spoon. Place artichokes in 1 quart of water to which 1 tablespoon lemon juice has been added. In food processor or blender, coarsely chop toasted almonds. Combine with next seven ingredients and 4 tablespoons oil. Drain artichokes. Divide stuffing equally among artichokes, filling center and pressing stuffing among leaves. Pour ½ cup water into a shallow, earthenware baking dish. Arrange artichokes in dish. Combine remaining 5 tablespoons oil and remaining 1 tablespoon lemon juice and drizzle over artichokes. Season with salt and pepper. Bake at 350° F. for 1 hour or until artichoke hearts are tender when pierced with a knife.
4 servings.

SPICED CANDIED EGGPLANT

Eggplants have an elusive quality that even staunch fans have trouble describing, while those who dislike or feel neutral about eggplant wonder what all the fuss is about. Often eggplant is poorly selected and even more poorly prepared. Large eggplants or eggplants past their prime are seedy and harsh tasting; eggplant cooked incorrectly is a disaster. Spiced Candied Eggplant seems to appeal to fans and nonfans alike. Its mélange of flavors and textures has its roots in Chinese cooking.

1 small eggplant, about 1 pound
½ teaspoon salt
¾ cup vegetable oil
1 clove garlic, chopped finely
¼ cup water
2 tablespoons soy sauce
2 tablespoons honey
¼ teaspoon red pepper flakes
⅓ cup Crystallized Almonds (page 174), chopped
2 tablespoons finely chopped, fresh cilantro

Cut the eggplant in ½-inch slices. Toss with salt and let sit in a colander for ½ hour. This step will draw out the bitter juices and reduce the amount of oil the eggplant absorbs. Blot eggplant with paper towels. In large skillet, lightly brown slices on both sides in hot oil. (Eggplant should not be fully cooked at this point.) Drain on paper towels. Pour any remaining oil out of pan. Return eggplant to pan. Mix garlic, water, soy sauce, honey, and red pepper flakes. Pour over eggplant. Bring to boil and cook until sauce reduces and caramelizes, about 3 to 5 minutes. Be careful not to burn. Arrange on serving platter. Just before serving, sprinkle with almonds and cilantro. Best served at room temperature.

6 servings.

MUSHROOMS STUFFED WITH GOAT CHEESE

Goat cheeses are an acquired taste that, once obtained, blossoms quickly into a passion. In the following recipe, the earthiness of the mushrooms and the cheese are a perfect pairing. Experiment with different types of goat cheeses. Some are quite strong while others are milder. For truly timid palates, substitute any mild, fresh, creamy cheese.

½ pound fresh, large mushrooms
½ cup chopped, natural almonds
7 tablespoons olive oil, divided
6 ounces goat cheese
1 clove garlic, chopped finely

1½ teaspoons chopped, fresh thyme or ½ teaspoon dried thyme
¼ teaspoon salt
¼ teaspoon freshly ground, white pepper

Remove stems from mushrooms, reserving caps, and chop finely. Sauté almonds in 1 tablespoon oil until crisp. Add chopped stems and cook 2 minutes, stirring constantly. Cool slightly. Mash goat cheese, and add 4 tablespoons oil, garlic, thyme, salt, and pepper, mixing well. Fold in almond mixture. Paint caps with remaining 2 tablespoons oil. Bake caps at 425° F. for 5 minutes. Fill with cheese mixture and continue baking 10 minutes longer or until cheese is hot and bubbly.
4 servings.

The first duty of a bell pepper is to be red—to paraphrase an old wine saying. Red bell peppers are simply green peppers that have been allowed to ripen on the plant. They are beautiful to look at and have an appealing sweet, peppery flavor. A bonus is that they don't seem to cause the same digestive problem that green peppers do for many people. The supply of red bell peppers is more erratic than that of green, but they are becoming more readily available as suppliers recognize the demand. Having said all that, honor demands that one say that this recipe works well with green peppers, although it takes a bit more cooking.

½ cup chopped, natural almonds
3 tablespoons olive oil, divided
2 tablespoons red wine vinegar
1 tablespoon Dijon mustard
2 large, red bell peppers, julienned
3 tablespoons finely sliced chives
⅛ teaspoon salt

Sauté almonds in 1 tablespoon oil until crisp; reserve. Combine vinegar and mustard; reserve. Sauté peppers in remaining 2 tablespoons oil, 2 to 3 minutes, until just tender. Add mustard mixture; cook 1 minute. Stir in chives, almonds, and salt.
4 servings.

HERB CHEESE TART

Pizza never seems to wane in popularity, perhaps because it keeps recreating itself in new guises. Some restaurants in California serve pizza with goat cheese and artichoke hearts — a trendy restaurant in Los Angeles even offers a truffled pizza. This version, called a tart to distinguish it from the pizza with a tomato sauce base, is not quite so luxurious but does boast the very compatible flavors of herbs, cheese, and almonds. The absence of sauce allows it to be cut easily into thin slivers to serve with drinks.

Dough

1 package, ¼ ounce, active dry yeast

½ cup warm (110° F) water

1½ cups flour, divided

½ teaspoon salt

2 tablespoons olive oil

Topping

1 clove garlic, chopped finely

1½ tablespoons olive oil, divided

¾ cup ricotta cheese

½ cup grated mozzarella cheese

½ cup grated Italian Fontina cheese

4 tablespoons freshly grated Parmesan cheese, divided

2 ounces prosciutto, chopped finely

½ tablespoon chopped, fresh basil or ¼ teaspoon dried basil

½ tablespoon chopped, fresh oregano or ¼ teaspoon dried oregano

½ cup blanched, slivered almonds, toasted

Combine yeast and water; let stand until completely dissolved, about 10 minutes. Meanwhile combine 1 cup flour, salt, and 2 tablespoons oil in bowl. Add yeast and water; mix 2 to 3 minutes. Add remaining ½ cup flour; turn out onto board and knead thoroughly into dough. Continue to knead dough 10 to 15 minutes or until dough is smooth and elastic. Lightly oil bowl and turn dough to coat with oil. Let rise in a warm place, covered, 1 hour or until doubled in volume. Punch dough down and spread into 10-inch tart pan with removable ring, pressing edges up the sides a bit. Or form into 10-inch circle on a cookie sheet. Let rise 1 hour or until doubled in volume. Mix garlic with ½ tablespoon oil and brush dough with mixture. Spread ricotta cheese on dough. Sprinkle top with mozzarella, Fontina, 2 tablespoons Parmesan, prosciutto, basil, and oregano. Lightly press almonds into topping. Sprinkle with remaining 2 tablespoons Parmesan cheese. Drizzle top with remaining 1 tablespoon oil. Bake at 425° F for 20 to 25 minutes or until crust is golden.

4 to 6 servings.

ALMOND GARLIC TOASTS

This country has been in a garlic frenzy for the past several years. In California alone, there is the Annual Garlic Festival, in Gilroy, the group called the Order of the Stinking Rose, and several restaurants that regularly celebrate this special member of the lily family. In certain circles it is considered terribly unchic to dislike garlic. This recipe uses a whole bulb. To the uninitiated, a whole bulb may seem extraordinary; yet the simmering of the unpeeled cloves develops a sweet and nutty flavor that pairs well with almonds. It is only when raw garlic is cut that the volatile oils oxidize and give off that distinctive odor.

1 whole bulb garlic (about 14 cloves)

7 teaspoons olive oil, divided

⅛ teaspoon salt

8 slices ½-inch-thick French bread (baguette style)

⅓ cup chopped, natural almonds, toasted

Separate bulb of garlic into cloves; simmer unpeeled, in lightly salted water, 15 minutes or until garlic cloves are soft. Drain and let cool. Peel garlic and mash until smooth. Blend in 3 teaspoons oil and salt. Toast one side of bread under broiler. Spread 1 teaspoon garlic paste on untoasted side of each slice of bread. Press garlic side of bread in toasted almonds. Place under broiler 1 to 2 minutes until heated. Drizzle ½ teaspoon of remaining oil over each slice.

4 servings.

CREAMED LEEK AND TOAST POINTS

In the past in France, leeks were referred to as the poor man's asparagus. Certainly, at their current price in this country, leeks are hardly poor man's fare. A member of the onion family, leeks have a sweet and delicate flavor and lend themselves to slow cooking, which caramelizes their natural sugars, intensifying a pleasant sweetness. Reduced cream makes this recipe an opulent introduction to an entrée of simple roasted veal or chicken.

1 cup heavy cream
½ cup chopped, natural almonds
3 tablespoons butter, divided
2 cups finely sliced leeks
½ teaspoon salt
¼ teaspoon freshly ground, white pepper

2 tablespoons chopped, fresh parsley
8 slices white bread, crust removed, toasted, and cut into triangles
1 bunch watercress, tough stems removed

Reduce cream by one-half and reserve. Sauté almonds in 1 tablespoon butter and reserve. Sauté leeks in remaining 2 tablespoons butter for 2 minutes. Cover and cook over low heat until leeks are soft but not colored. Stir in cream, almonds, salt, pepper, and parsley. Serve with toast points and watercress.

4 servings.

FETA AND FENNEL TOASTS

Nowadays, feta can be made from either sheep, goat, or cow's milk. Some are salty, sharp, and crumbly, while others are milder and creamier. The latter works best for this recipe. A summer variation — dice the cheese, marinate it, toss with almonds, and serve it as a first course next to thick slices of luscious, red tomato.

¾ cup chopped, natural almonds

8 tablespoons olive oil, divided

½ pound feta cheese

1 tablespoon fennel seeds, crushed

1 teaspoon whole black peppercorns, crushed

12 to 16 slices French bread (baguette style)

Sauté almonds in 1 tablespoon oil until crisp; reserve. Mash feta cheese. Mix in fennel seeds, peppercorns, and remaining 7 tablespoons oil. Marinate 1 hour. Fold in almonds. Toast one side of bread under broiler. Spread about 1 tablespoon mixture on untoasted side of each bread slice. Broil until cheese begins to bubble, about 3 minutes.

4 to 6 servings.

ALMOND SHRIMP TOASTS

Secretly and not so secretly, many of us love rich, fried, little tidbits. These toasts are a version of a hot Chinese appetizer, and are the kind of sturdy morsel that people devour with drinks. They are easy to make, can be multiplied for a party, and prove, once again, what a fine marriage almonds and shrimp make.

⅔ cup blanched, whole almonds, toasted

⅓ pound shrimp, shelled and deveined

1 green onion, sliced (including green)

1 tablespoon lemon juice

1 teaspoon grated, fresh ginger or ¼ teaspoon powdered ginger

½ teaspoon salt

¼ teaspoon sugar

1 egg white, beaten

Pinch cayenne

8 thin slices two-day-old white bread, crusts removed

Vegetable oil for frying

In food processor, finely grind almonds. Remove half the almonds and reserve. With machine running, add next eight ingredients, one at a time, to remaining almonds. (To prepare by hand, finely grind almonds in blender. Remove half the almonds and reserve. Transfer remaining almonds to a bowl. Add finely chopped shrimp, chopped green onion, lemon juice, ginger, salt, sugar, beaten egg white, and cayenne.) Spread bread with shrimp mixture. Press coated side in reserved ground almonds. Cut each slice of bread into two triangles. In one-inch of oil, fry toasts, shrimp-side down, until golden. Turn, brown the other side and drain.

8 servings.

SPAGHETTI WITH ALMONDS

Pasta is the perfect grown-up answer to the occasional craving for warm, soft, starchy food—what James Beard calls nursery food. This recipe can be made quickly and easily yet consists of sophisticated flavors that act as a counterpoint to the basic comforting warmth and texture. This dish is very satisfying eaten out of individual bowls at midnight. As a prelude to a charcoal grilled steak, it is both delicious and chic.

⅔ cup chopped, natural almonds
6 tablespoons olive oil, divided
3 tablespoons freshly grated, Parmesan cheese
3 cloves garlic, chopped finely
2 tablespoons chopped, fresh parsley
8 ounces spaghetti
1 tablespoon butter
½ teaspoon salt
½ teaspoon red pepper flakes
¼ teaspoon freshly ground, black pepper
Pinch freshly grated nutmeg

Sauté almonds in 1 tablespoon oil until crisp; reserve. Combine remaining 5 tablespoons oil, cheese, and garlic. Fold in parsley; reserve. Cook spaghetti in salted, boiling water until just tender. Drain. Toss with butter, salt, red pepper, black pepper, and nutmeg. Then toss with the cheese mixture. Stir in almonds.

4 servings.

PASTA WITH MUSTARD AND MINT

The popularity of pasta has bred its own excesses—and, certainly, chocolate-flavored pasta seems to be one. On the other hand, one of pasta's endearing qualities is its readiness to absorb an endless variety of flavors.

For those of us brought up on spaghetti with tomato sauce, there is a certain, heady freedom in pasta with artichokes or goat cheese and herbs. This recipe combines mustard and mint in a compound butter that complements the sweet crunchiness of the almonds.

⅔ cup chopped, natural almonds

½ cup + 1 tablespoon butter, softened, divided

2 tablespoons Dijon mustard

2 tablespoons chopped, fresh parsley

1 tablespoon chopped, fresh mint or 1 teaspoon dried mint

8 ounces fresh fettuccine

Sauté almonds in 1 tablespoon butter until crisp; reserve. Combine remaining ½ cup butter, mustard, parsley, and mint; reserve. Cook the pasta in salted, boiling water until tender; drain. Return to pan and stir in the mustard-butter, a little at a time, over low heat. Fold in almonds.

4 servings.

PASTA WITH ARTICHOKES

In many parts of the country, little, fresh artichokes no bigger than a large thumb are available in Italian grocery stores or specialty food stores. The choke has not yet formed, and the whole artichoke is edible after trimming the tips and the tough outer leaves. While fresh artichokes are preferred, frozen artichoke hearts make an adequate alternative.

12 tiny, fresh artichokes (1 package, 9 ounces, frozen artichoke hearts may be substituted)

1 lemon, halved

1 onion, chopped

1 tablespoon butter

2 cloves garlic, chopped finely

½ cup white wine

1 cup heavy cream

8 ounces fresh fettuccine, white, green or mixed, cooked

⅔ cup chopped, natural almonds, toasted

½ cup freshly grated, Parmesan cheese

For fresh artichokes, trim stem, remove tough outer leaves, and top. Cut in halves (or quarter, if large). Rub with ½ lemon; reserve. (Defrost frozen artichoke hearts and use just as they come in the package.) Sauté onion in butter until translucent. Add garlic, then white wine, the juice of remaining ½ lemon, and fresh or thawed artichokes; cover and cook over medium heat, 1 to 2 minutes. Add cream and cook, uncovered, 2 to 3 minutes longer until mixture thickens slightly. Add pasta, almonds, and cheese; toss and serve.

4 servings.

FETTUCCINE GORGONZOLA

Blue cheese, the generic term that includes some of the world's greatest cheeses—for example; Roquefort, Stilton, Gorgonzola—seems to invite extremes of passion. The distinctive bite of the blue mold varies in intensity and style depending on the type of cheese. Gorgonzola appeals to the lover of blue cheese and blends well with the pasta and almonds in this recipe. Other cheeses in the blue family may be substituted at the discretion of the cook.

¾ cup chopped, natural almonds

1 tablespoon olive oil

8 ounces fresh fettuccine

1 cup heavy cream

6 ounces Gorgonzola cheese, crumbled

1 tablespoon amontillado (medium) sherry

¼ teaspoon freshly ground, white pepper

2 tablespoons chopped, fresh parsley

Sauté almonds in oil until crisp; reserve. Plunge fettuccine into salted, boiling water and cook until just tender. While pasta is cooking, reduce cream by one-half. Add cheese and cook over low heat, stirring constantly, until cheese melts. Add sherry and pepper and cook 1 minute. Toss hot, drained pasta with sauce, almonds, and parsley. 4 servings.

SCALLOPS AND SPINACH FETTUCCINE WITH CURRY SAUCE

Good fresh pasta has a fine, silky texture that feels wonderful in the mouth and absorbs flavors even better than the dried version. Fresh pasta is becoming increasingly available in specialty food shops and even some supermarkets. Cookbooks and magazines abound with pasta recipes that are simple to make by hand or that practically make themselves in any pasta machine. This recipe pairs the delectable sweetness of scallops with fresh, green fettuccine in a light, curried, cream sauce. It's an engaging first course for something like a grilled veal chop or a delightful light supper before or after the theater.

¾ cup blanched, slivered almonds

3 tablespoons olive oil, divided

¼ cup flour

1 teaspoon salt, divided

1 pound scallops (if large, slice into medallions)

3 tablespoons butter, divided

2 tablespoons finely chopped shallots

1 clove garlic, chopped finely

¼ cup dry vermouth

1½ cups heavy cream

½ teaspoon freshly ground, white pepper

½ teaspoon curry powder

8 ounces fresh, spinach fettuccine

¼ teaspoon lemon juice

¼ cup thinly sliced chives

Sauté almonds in 1 tablespoon oil; reserve. Mix flour and ½ teaspoon salt; dredge scallops in mixture, shaking off excess. Sauté scallops in remaining 2 tablespoons oil and 2 tablespoons butter over medium-high heat until golden, about 2 minutes. Remove and keep warm. Sauté shallots and garlic for 30 seconds in the fat remaining in the pan. Deglaze with vermouth and cook 1 minute. Add cream, remaining ½ teaspoon salt, pepper, and curry powder and reduce by half or until sauce thickens and coats the back of a spoon. While sauce reduces, cook fettuccine in salted, boiling water until tender. Drain and toss with remaining 1 tablespoon butter. Stir lemon juice and scallops into sauce. Toss hot noodles with sauce and almonds. Sprinkle with chives.

4 to 6 servings.

SHRIMP AND NOODLES WITH GINGER VINAIGRETTE

Shrimp and almonds have a natural affinity for each other and combine especially well in this dish that has its roots in Chinese cuisine. The bean threads, often referred to as cellophane noodles, glass noodles or transparent noodles, can be purchased in Oriental specialty food stores or in supermarkets in cities that have a sizable Asian population. Clear and rather slippery in texture, bean threads do not appeal to everyone. Vermicelli is a workable substitute, although it changes the delicate nature of the dish.

¾ pound medium, raw shrimp, shelled and deveined

1 tablespoon lemon juice

1½ teaspoons red pepper flakes, divided

⅓ cup blanched, slivered almonds

½ cup + 1 tablespoon vegetable oil

¼ cup rice vinegar

1 teaspoon honey

1 teaspoon salt

1 clove garlic, chopped finely

½ teaspoon grated, fresh ginger or ⅛ teaspoon powdered ginger

3½ ounces bean threads

½ cup thinly sliced green onions, including green, divided

4 teaspoons finely chopped, crystallized ginger

Place shrimp in a saucepan and just cover with hot water. Stir in lemon juice and 1 teaspoon red pepper flakes. Bring to a boil, reduce heat, and simmer 1 minute. Drain and plunge into ice water. Let cool. Drain. Cut shrimp in half lengthwise and reserve. Sauté almonds in 1 tablespoon oil until golden; reserve. Combine vinegar, honey, salt, garlic, ginger, and remaining ½ teaspoon red pepper flakes. Beat in remaining ½ cup oil. Add shrimp to dressing and allow to marinate several hours in the refrigerator. Just before serving, prepare noodles. Cover noodles with boiling water and let sit 10 minutes or until noodles are just tender. Drain and reserve. Drain shrimp and reserve dressing. Toss noodles with dressing and one-half the onions. Arrange noodles on a serving dish. Sprinkle with crystallized ginger. Arrange shrimp on top. Top with remaining onions and almonds.

4 to 6 servings.

LAMB MEATBALLS

Tiny meatballs have suffered a great deal of abuse in their execution. They are often overcooked until they resemble hard little knots, and then engulfed in a floury, brown sauce. Being speared on cocktail picks can be the final indignity. For best results, use a light hand when forming meatballs and handle as little as possible. Cook until just done—a bit of pink in the center is fine. The result is flavorful and juicy. In this version of curry-scented lamb meatballs, ground almonds replace the usual bread crumbs and add a special flavor and texture. Finally, these savory morsels are marinated in a lemon vinaigrette flavored with oregano. A plateful of meatballs with crusty, peasant bread is wonderful. You can even spear them.

Meatballs

1 cup blanched, whole almonds, toasted

1 pound lean, ground lamb

1 egg

1 tablespoon curry powder

1 teaspoon ground cumin

Pinch cinnamon

4 cloves garlic, chopped finely

¾ teaspoon salt

Sauce

2 tablespoons lemon juice

1 clove garlic, chopped finely

1½ teaspoons chopped, fresh oregano or ½ teaspoon dried oregano

¼ teaspoon salt

⅛ teaspoon freshly ground, black pepper

6 tablespoons olive oil, divided

Finely chop almonds. Mix with next seven ingredients. Form into 1-inch balls and chill. Meanwhile, prepare sauce by mixing lemon juice, garlic, oregano, salt, and pepper. Gradually beat in 4 tablespoons oil and reserve. Brown meatballs in remaining 2 tablespoons oil; take care not to overcook. Drain. Mix with reserved sauce. Marinate at least 1 hour. Serve at room temperature.

6 servings.

BAKED MUSSELS WITH ALMONDS AND PERNOD

Fresh mussels are available all year, although easier to find at certain times. It is essential that they be well-scrubbed with a stiff brush in cold water. Discard any that are broken or opened. Next, use scissors or a sharp knife to cut away the beard and proceed with cooking. In this recipe, the flavors of almonds and Pernod marry deliciously with the sea tastes of the mussels. The mussels may be prepared several hours ahead, just shy of baking, allowing an unruffled cook to produce an elegant first course.

Coarse salt

½ cup whole, blanched almonds, toasted and chopped coarsely

6 tablespoons chopped, fresh parsley

6 tablespoons butter, softened

4 cloves garlic, chopped finely

2 tablespoons lemon juice

1½ tablespoons Pernod

¼ teaspoon salt

2½ dozen large, fresh mussels, cleaned

Fill four individual gratin dishes with coarse salt; reserve. Combine next seven ingredients; reserve. Place mussels in heavy saucepan. Cover and cook over high heat, shaking twice, for 3 to 4 minutes or until all mussels open. (Discard any unopened mussels.) Cool. Remove mussels from shell, reserving the deep half of shell for each mussel. Wash shells. Place one mussel on each shell. Spread a teaspoon or more of butter mixture over each mussel on the half shell. Arrange 6 mussels in each oven-proof dish. Bake at 500° F. for 3 to 5 minutes or until mussels are hot and topping begins to brown.

4 servings.

GRATIN OF SNAILS

There is no discussing snails. Like raw oysters, one either does or does not eat them. It is the notion of eating snails and oysters that must be acquired, other than the taste. For those who have acquired the taste, Gratin of Snails is a savory change from the ubiquitous à la bourguignonne of the typical French-ified restaurant in the United States. For those who would like to acquire the taste, a blanket of toasted almonds and bread crumbs, seasoned with ginger, mustard, and lime, might suggest the way.

½ cup whole, natural almonds, toasted

12 snails, rinsed and dried

4 tablespoons butter, divided

1 shallot, chopped finely

1 clove garlic, chopped finely

1 teaspoon grated, fresh ginger or ¼ teaspoon powdered ginger

¼ cup dry white wine

1 teaspoon Dijon mustard

2 tablespoons fresh, white bread crumbs

2 tablespoons heavy cream

1 tablespoon chopped, fresh parsley

1 teaspoon lime juice

½ teaspoon salt

¼ teaspoon freshly ground, white pepper

¼ teaspoon sugar

Coarsely chop almonds in food processor or blender; reserve. Sauté snails for 30 seconds in 1 tablespoon butter. Remove and reserve. Sauté shallots, garlic, and ginger in 1 tablespoon butter until shallots are translucent. Add wine and mustard; cook over high heat 1 minute. Remove from heat. Add remaining 2 tablespoons butter. Mix with almonds. Blend in remaining ingredients. Divide snails among four individual, shallow baking dishes. Divide topping in same manner. Bake at 550° F. for 5 minutes until snails are heated through and topping is bubbly.

4 servings.

ORANGE SLICES AND ALMONDS WITH GARLIC

Here's a version of an Italian salad that may seem an odd combination of flavors to those not familiar with it. Be assured that the oranges, olive oil, and garlic work beautifully together. The crunch and flavor of toasted almonds add a new dimension. This recipe is excellent with poultry or pork.

3 navel oranges, peeled and sliced

2 tablespoons olive oil

2 cloves garlic, chopped finely

1 teaspoon sugar

¼ teaspoon salt

⅛ teaspoon freshly ground, white pepper

½ cup sliced, natural almonds, toasted

Arrange oranges on platter. Drizzle with oil. Sprinkle with garlic, sugar, salt, and pepper. Cover with plastic wrap and chill several hours. Just before serving, sprinkle top with almonds.

4 servings.

GOAT CHEESE, PAPAYA, AND WATERCRESS SALAD

Watercress is underrated as a salad ingredient, but its deep green color and intense, peppery flavor make it an interesting addition. In this recipe, watercress combines with the sweet muskiness of papaya and the rich bite of goat cheese. This salad can either start a meal, California-style, or be served after the main course.

3 tablespoons white wine vinegar
¼ teaspoon salt
   Pinch freshly ground, black pepper
6 tablespoons olive oil
⅔ cup sliced, natural almonds, toasted

1 papaya, peeled and sliced
4 ounces goat cheese, crumbled
4 bunches watercress, tough stems removed

Combine vinegar, salt, and pepper; beat in oil. Gently toss almonds, papaya, and goat cheese with 2 tablespoons of dressing. Toss watercress with remaining dressing. Divide watercress among 4 plates. Top each plate with almond mixture.
4 servings.

APPLE AND WATERCRESS SALAD

Sautéed almonds, tart green apples, and the bite of watercress are united in a mustard-laced vinaigrette. A fruit salad for those who find Waldorf Salad insipid.

¾ cup chopped, natural almonds

⅓ cup + 1 tablespoon olive oil

1 tablespoon white wine vinegar

1 teaspoon Dijon mustard

¼ teaspoon salt

¼ teaspoon freshly ground, white pepper

2 crisp, red, eating apples, unpeeled

1 bunch watercress, tough stems removed

Sauté almonds in 1 tablespoon oil until crisp; reserve. Combine vinegar, mustard, salt, and pepper. Beat in remaining ⅓ cup oil. Core apples and julienne. Immediately add to dressing. Toss almonds and watercress with apples.

4 servings.

GRAPE AND WATERCRESS SALAD

The peppery taste of watercress and the sweet acidity of green grapes make a lively salad that works well with rich meats such as pork or duck. The chile powder in the vinaigrette adds a surprise piquant note.

2 tablespoons lemon juice

1 clove garlic, chopped finely

¼ teaspoon salt

½ teaspoon chile powder

½ teaspoon sugar

6 tablespoons olive oil

2 cups seedless, green grapes, cut in half lengthwise

½ cup blanched, slivered almonds, toasted

2 bunches watercress, tough stems removed

Combine first five ingredients; beat in oil. Toss grapes, almonds, and watercress with dressing.

4 servings.

Orange and red onion salad has become a classic of sorts. In this version, toasted almonds and a piquant, herb vinaigrette complement the sweetness of the fruit and the bite of the onion. Serve it before or after rich meats and game. The addition of slivers of chicken or duck breast could convert it to a fine, light luncheon dish.

⅔ cup chopped, natural almonds

¼ cup + 1 tablespoon olive oil, divided

2 large navel oranges, peeled and sectioned, free of membrane

1 medium red onion, sliced thinly and separated into rings

2 tablespoons white wine

1 teaspoon finely chopped, fresh thyme or ¼ teaspoon dried thyme

½ teaspoon sugar

½ teaspoon salt

¼ teaspoon finely chopped garlic

¼ teaspoon cumin

¼ teaspoon freshly ground, white pepper

Sauté almonds in 1 tablespoon oil until crisp; reserve. Arrange orange sections and onion slices on plate. Combine next seven ingredients and beat in remaining ¼ cup oil. Sprinkle almonds over salad and drizzle with dressing.

4 to 6 servings.

GREEN BEAN SALAD

A tart, fresh-tasting green bean and almond salad proves the versatility of this classic combination. The red pepper flakes add a judicious spark of fire.

1 pound green beans, trimmed and
   sliced diagonally in 1-inch pieces

1 tablespoon lemon juice

¾ teaspoon salt

¼ teaspoon freshly ground, black
   pepper

¼ teaspoon red pepper flakes

½ cup blanched, slivered almonds

3 tablespoons olive oil

Plunge green beans into salted, boiling water and cook until just tender. Drain and refresh in cold water. Green beans should be crisp and bright green. Mix lemon juice, salt, pepper, and pepper flakes; reserve. Sauté almonds in oil until golden; remove from heat and add lemon juice mixture. Toss with green beans. Serve at room temperature.
4 servings.

WARM RED CABBAGE SALAD

This warm, red cabbage salad is a feast for the senses. Visually beautiful, it boasts a beguiling interplay of textures, flavors, and temperatures. Serve it as a light meal, a first course or a tart balance to the richness of pork or duck.

¾ cup chopped, natural almonds

4 tablespoons olive oil, divided

1 pound red cabbage, sliced ½-inch thick

2 tablespoons red wine vinegar

½ teaspoon salt

4 ounces cold goat cheese, crumbled

¼ teaspoon freshly ground, black pepper

Sauté almonds in 1 tablespoon oil until crisp; reserve. Add remaining 3 tablespoons oil to pan and sauté cabbage until just tender. Stir in vinegar and salt and cook over high heat, stirring, for 1 minute. Stir in almonds. Transfer cabbage to serving plate. Sprinkle with goat cheese, then pepper.

4 to 6 servings.

CELERY AND BLUE CHEESE SALAD

In a gentler age, celery often was passed with pickles and olives on a relish tray at the beginning of dinner. Dining has become less formal, but here's a pungent celery and blue cheese salad that makes a lively beginning to a meal. It is particularly tasty as a prelude to grilled steak.

1 cup chopped, natural almonds

6 tablespoons olive oil, divided

4 ounces blue cheese

1 tablespoon brandy

1 tablespoon white wine vinegar

3 cups thinly sliced celery hearts

Sauté almonds in 1 tablespoon oil until crisp; reserve. Mash cheese with brandy and vinegar. Beat in remaining 5 tablespoons oil. Mix dressing with celery. Chill. Just before serving, fold in almonds.

6 to 8 servings.

WARM SPINACH SALAD WITH ALMONDS

In this simple but well-balanced spinach salad, the hot, sherry-laced vinaigrette permeates and perfumes the sturdy spinach. The leaves glisten and have a translucent quality that is quite beautiful.

1 bunch fresh spinach

1 cup sliced, natural almonds

¼ cup olive oil

2 tablespoons sherry vinegar

½ tablespoon dry sherry

¼ teaspoon salt

Pinch freshly ground, black pepper

Wash spinach thoroughly and remove stems; dry and reserve. Sauté almonds in oil until golden. Stir in vinegar and dry sherry. Season with salt and pepper. Pour hot dressing over spinach and toss.

4 servings.

EGGPLANT-APPLE SALAD

This unusual salad combines egg-plant and apple in a savory, spicy, vinegar and oil dressing. The intense and intriguing spectrum of flavors makes this a marvelous beginning for a hearty meal or a fine substitute for the ubiquitous potato salad at a barbecue.

1 eggplant, unpeeled, and diced

1¼ teaspoons salt, divided

1 cup blanched, slivered almonds

6 tablespoons olive oil, divided

2 tablespoons finely chopped shallots

1 tablespoon red wine vinegar

1 tablespoon tomato paste

1 tablespoon plum jam

1 teaspoon Dijon mustard

1 clove garlic, chopped finely

¾ teaspoon red pepper flakes

¼ teaspoon freshly ground, black pepper

1 red onion, sliced

1 crisp, eating apple, peeled, cored, and diced

½ cup raisins, soaked in boiling water for 20 minutes and drained

¼ cup chopped, fresh parsley

Toss eggplant with ½ teaspoon salt and let drain in colander ½ hour. Meanwhile, sauté almonds in 1 tablespoon oil until golden; reserve. Combine shallots, vinegar, tomato paste, jam, mustard, garlic, red pepper flakes, black pepper, and remaining ¾ teaspoon salt. Beat in 2 tablespoons oil; reserve. Blot eggplant dry with paper towel, and sauté in 2 tablespoons oil over medium heat until golden. Remove from heat and reserve. Add remaining 1 tablespoon oil to pan and sauté onions until translucent. Add apples and sauté until just tender. Mix with eggplant, raisins, and parsley. Pour dressing over and toss gently. Cool. Chill several hours to marry flavors. Bring to room temperature, and just before serving, fold in almonds.

6 to 8 servings.

38

VEGETABLE MELANGE MARINATED IN MUSTARD VINAIGRETTE

Here's a colorful, crunchy combination of vegetables marinated in a spicy, sweet vinaigrette. Use it as a fine, light first course or a cheerful change from coleslaw.

¾ cup chopped, natural almonds

7 tablespoons vegetable oil, divided

1 tablespoon Dijon mustard

1 tablespoon brown sugar

2 tablespoons rice vinegar

½ teaspoon salt

½ teaspoon freshly ground, black pepper

2 tablespoons Oriental sesame oil

1 cup julienned celery

1 cup julienned carrots

1 medium red bell pepper, julienned

Sauté almonds in 1 tablespoon vegetable oil until crisp; reserve. Combine mustard, sugar, vinegar, salt, and pepper. Beat in sesame oil and remaining 6 tablespoons vegetable oil. Toss the vegetables with the dressing. Chill several hours. Just before serving, fold in almonds.

4 to 6 servings.

RED NEW POTATO SALAD

Lime, cumin, and crunchy, stylishly julienned vegetables give this perennial favorite a new dimension. Be certain to use red, new potatoes; baking potatoes are too starchy and mealy for salads.

1 cup chopped, natural almonds

¼ cup + 1 tablespoon olive oil, divided

2 tablespoons lime juice

1 teaspoon salt

¼ teaspoon freshly ground, white pepper

¼ teaspoon sugar

¼ teaspoon ground cumin

¼ cup mayonnaise

1½ pounds small, red, new potatoes, steamed and sliced

½ cup sliced green onion

½ cup julienned red bell pepper

½ cup julienned celery

1 tablespoon chopped, fresh cilantro

Sauté almonds in 1 tablespoon oil until crisp; reserve. Combine next six ingredients. Gradually beat in remaining ¼ cup oil. Gently toss with potatoes. Fold in green onion, bell pepper, celery, and cilantro. Chill. Just before serving, fold in almonds. 6 to 8 servings.

Almond butter thickens and enriches the dressing for this cold noodle salad. Inspired by the cuisines of Southeast Asia, this colorful dish is a perfect light meal and a welcome change from chicken salad, with mayonnaise and celery.

¼ cup + 2 tablespoons loosely packed, fresh cilantro leaves, divided

½ cup almond butter (see On Almonds)

⅓ cup soy sauce

¼ cup dry sherry

¼ cup sugar

3 cloves garlic

1 tablespoon lime juice

½ teaspoon red pepper flakes

4 ounces vermicelli, cooked and drained

2 whole chicken breasts, skinned, boned, poached, and cut into strips

½ cup sliced green onions

½ cup sliced celery

½ cup diced red bell pepper

Romaine lettuce

Finely chop 2 tablespoons cilantro leaves and reserve. Purée next seven ingredients and remaining ¼ cup cilantro leaves in food processor or blender until smooth. Toss with noodles, chicken, green onions, celery, bell pepper, and chopped cilantro. Serve on a bed of romaine lettuce.

4 servings.

CHINESE-STYLE ALMOND PASTA

For most of us, our introduction to Chinese food was the rice-based cuisine of southern China. In fact, noodles are an important and popular part of the Chinese diet. This salad, inspired by a love of things Chinese, is pungent with hoisin sauce, a spicy sweet, fermented bean paste that is addictive. It, along with toasted sesame oil, is available in Oriental markets or even some supermarkets.

Chinese-Style Almond Pasta is perfect for a picnic or barbecue. It also makes an unusual first course, accompanied by chopsticks for the proper mood.

8 ounces Chinese egg noodles (spaghetti may be substituted)

6 tablespoons hoisin sauce

3 tablespoons soy sauce

3 tablespoons Oriental sesame oil, divided

2 tablespoons rice vinegar

2 cups chopped, natural almonds, toasted

3 cloves garlic, chopped finely

1 teaspoon grated, fresh ginger or ¼ teaspoon powdered ginger

1 cup diagonally sliced green onions

Cook pasta in salted, boiling water until tender. Meanwhile, combine hoisin sauce, soy sauce, 1 tablespoon sesame oil, and vinegar; reserve. When pasta is done, drain and toss with sauce. Arrange on platter. Sauté almonds, garlic, ginger, and green onions in remaining 2 tablespoons sesame oil, stirring occasionally, 2 to 3 minutes or until onions are just tender. Spoon almond mixture over pasta.

6 to 8 servings.

GRILLED EGGPLANT PASTA SALAD

Pasta salads have been quite the rage the last few years—with good reason. They take advantage of pasta's marvelous ability to absorb flavors, are easy to prepare, and address themselves to a healthy diet. This version boasts smoky bits of grilled eggplant; tart, diced tomato; and chopped spicy green olives. This eggplant pasta salad, along with a few curls of the very best ham, some buffalo mozzarella, crusty bread, and a jug of red wine would make a perfect picnic.

1 eggplant, about 1½ pounds
3¾ teaspoons salt, divided
5 tablespoons olive oil, divided
8 ounces corkscrew (fusilli) pasta
2 cloves garlic, chopped finely
¾ teaspoon red pepper flakes
½ cup diced onion
1½ cups peeled, seeded, and diced tomatoes, drained
¾ cup blanched, slivered almonds, toasted
½ cup chopped, spiced green olives
1 tablespoon red wine vinegar

Slice eggplant ½-inch thick. Sprinkle slices with 3 teaspoons salt; drain 20 minutes on paper towels. Wipe slices dry. Brush one side of eggplant slices with 1½ teaspoons oil; broil 10 minutes or until golden. Turn slices and brush with another 1½ teaspoons oil; broil 10 minutes more or until golden. Dice eggplant; reserve. Cook pasta in salted, boiling water until just tender. Drain and return to pan. Add eggplant, garlic, and pepper flakes; cover and reserve. Sauté onion in remaining 4 tablespoons oil until translucent. Stir onion, remaining ¾ teaspoon salt, tomatoes, almonds, olives, and vinegar into pasta.

6 to 8 servings.

MEXICAN-STYLE ALMOND CHICKEN SALAD

This spicy, Mexican-style chicken salad served in a crisp, flour tortilla gains high marks for flavor, texture, and visual appeal. All the components can be prepared ahead and assembled just before serving. Dry, homemade sangría or Mexican beer should accompany this dish.

2 whole chicken breasts, skinned, boned, cut in half, and poached

1 cup blanched, slivered almonds

⅓ cup + 2 teaspoons vegetable oil, divided

6 tablespoons lime juice

3 cloves garlic, chopped finely

5 teaspoons ground cumin

⅛ teaspoon cayenne

½ teaspoon salt

6 tablespoons mayonnaise

1 small red onion, chopped

2 oranges, peeled and diced

4 flour tortillas

Vegetable oil for frying

Garnish

Lettuce leaves

Avocado, sliced

Orange, peeled and sliced

Red onion rings

Blanched, slivered almonds, toasted

Cut chicken into 1-inch cubes; reserve. Sauté almonds in 2 teaspoons oil until golden; reserve. Combine lime juice, garlic, cumin, cayenne, and salt. Beat in mayonnaise and remaining ⅓ cup oil. Add chicken, onion, and almonds. Gently fold in oranges. Fry tortillas in oil, one at a time, turning once, until crisp, puffed, and golden; drain and reserve. (A ladle can be pressed in the center of the tortilla while frying to form shell.) To serve, line each tortilla with lettuce leaves and top with one-fourth chicken salad. Garnish each serving with avocado slices, slice of orange, and onion rings. Garnish each serving with almonds.

4 servings.

CHINESE-STYLE ALMOND CHICKEN SALAD

An Oriental-inspired chicken salad is a fresh alternative to the usual mayonnaise and celery concoction. The intense flavor of toasted sesame oil enhances the nuttiness of the almonds, and the richness of both contrasts deliciously with the crisp, fresh vegetables and the pungent seasoning.

3 tablespoons rice vinegar

1 tablespoon soy sauce

1 tablespoon honey

1 teaspoon grated, fresh ginger or ¼ teaspoon powdered ginger

½ teaspoon salt

3 tablespoons Oriental sesame oil

2 tablespoons vegetable oil

2 whole chicken breasts, skinned, boned, poached, and julienned

1 cucumber, peeled, seeded, and sliced

1 cup sliced radishes

½ cup sliced green onion

1 cup blanched, slivered almonds, toasted

Mix vinegar, soy sauce, honey, ginger, and salt. Beat in oils. Pour dressing over chicken, cucumber, radishes, and green onion, and toss. Chill. Just before serving, fold in almonds.

4 servings.

CRAB SALAD WITH BELGIAN ENDIVE AND KIWI FRUIT

Kiwi fruit and freshly grated ginger spark the rich sweetness of crab in this salad influenced by the new California cuisine. The crab must be faultless; short of that, substitute the very best shrimp or scallops, gently poached.

2 tablespoons lemon juice

¾ teaspoon salt

2 pinches cayenne

1 egg yolk

¾ cup vegetable oil

1 tablespoon finely chopped shallots

½ teaspoon grated, fresh ginger or
⅛ teaspoon powdered ginger

8 ounces cleaned crab meat

1 cup kiwi fruit, peeled, quartered, and sliced ¼-inch thick

½ cup blanched, slivered almonds, toasted

12 Belgian endive leaves

Mix lemon juice, salt, and cayenne. Beat in egg yolk. Slowly beat in oil. Gently fold in shallots, ginger, crab meat, kiwi, and almonds. Take care not to overmix. Garnish four plates with endive leaves and top with crab salad.

4 servings.

WARM PORK AND VEGETABLE SALAD

Warm salads have been much the vogue in recent years. The warming of the ingredients releases flavors and aromas and allows them to marry in a way not possible in chilled dishes. This Oriental-inspired version is a burst of color and varied texture in a piquant, hoisin-spiked dressing. The pork bits add substance and make it suitable for a light meal. Divided in a greater number of portions, it's a fine appetizer. All preparation should be made ahead, and everything should be measured and at hand. Once the cooking starts, things move rapidly.

2 tablespoons hoisin sauce

2 tablespoons red wine vinegar

1 tablespoon soy sauce

¾ teaspoon salt

3 tablespoons vegetable oil, divided

1 red bell pepper, julienned

6 green onions, sliced (reserve green portion for garnish)

2 cloves garlic, chopped finely

½ carrot, julienned

½ pound pork tenderloin, cut into strips (pork top loin may be substituted)

¼ pound snow peas, blanched

½ teaspoon red pepper flakes

½ cup whole, natural almonds, toasted

4 cups torn, mixed salad greens (such as curly endive, green leaf lettuce, romaine, butter lettuce)

Combine first four ingredients; reserve. In 2 tablespoons oil, sauté bell pepper for 3 minutes. Add green onions and garlic; cook 1 minute longer. Remove vegetables; reserve. In oil remaining in pan, sauté carrots 2 minutes. Remove and reserve. Add remaining 1 tablespoon oil and sauté pork over high heat until brown. Return sautéed vegetables to pan; add snow peas, pepper flakes, soy sauce mixture, and almonds. Cook 1 minute. Toss with salad greens. Garnish with sliced green onion tops. 4 servings.

WARM STEAK SALAD WITH LEMON AND PEPPER

Here's a hearty, warm beef salad inspired by the cuisines of Southeast Asia. The bits of diced lemon with peel and the red pepper flakes add a lively piquancy to the richness of the beef.

3 tablespoons honey

2 cloves garlic, chopped finely

1 pound flank steak, sliced thinly

⅔ cup chopped, natural almonds

4 tablespoons olive oil

½ lemon, including peel, diced

¾ teaspoon red pepper flakes

¾ teaspoon salt

3 to 4 bunches watercress, tough stems removed

Combine honey and garlic; toss with steak. Allow to marinate at room temperature for 1 hour. Sauté almonds in oil 2 minutes. Add steak and sauté over high heat, 3 to 4 minutes or until steak is browned and almonds are crisp. Take care not to overcook. Add lemon, pepper flakes, and salt. Remove from heat. Toss with watercress. 4 servings.

ALMOND CURRIED TUNA SALAD

This zesty tuna salad quickly overcomes memories of those dreary, celery-laden mixtures of childhood and coffee shop fame. The fruit and almonds add a delicious texture and act as counterpoints to the curry flavors. Alternatively, try this mixture on thick slices of egg bread and reassess your stance on tuna sandwiches.

¼ cup blanched, slivered almonds

1 teaspoon vegetable oil

¼ cup mayonnaise

2 tablespoons plain yogurt

1 teaspoon curry powder

¼ teaspoon salt

1 clove garlic, chopped finely

2 tablespoons raisins, soaked in boiling water for 20 minutes and drained

1 green apple, unpeeled, cored, and diced

4 green onions, sliced

1 stalk celery, sliced

1 can (7 ounces), water-packed, white tuna, drained

Lettuce

Apple slices dipped in lemon juice

Sauté almonds in oil until golden; reserve. Combine next five ingredients. Stir in raisins, apple, green onion, and celery. Fold tuna into salad. Do not overmix. Chill. Just before serving, fold in almonds. Divide salad mixture among four lettuce-lined plates; garnish each serving with apple slices.

4 servings.

MUSTARD-GLAZED TURNIPS

At best, people are indifferent to turnips. At worst, the harsh, woody, oversized vegetables that are so prevalent in the markets have generated strong dislike. Select small, fresh-looking turnips for this sweet and spicy sauté. Dijon mustard, brown sugar, and almonds are the perfect foil for the mild bite of the turnip. This dish may well create some converts. Tell them they are eating turnips after they taste.

¼ cup firmly packed, dark brown sugar
2 tablespoons Dijon mustard
½ teaspoon salt
½ teaspoon freshly ground, white pepper

2 pounds small, white turnips, about 5, peeled and julienned
⅔ cup chopped, natural almonds
3 tablespoons butter, divided
1 tablespoon vegetable oil

Combine first four ingredients and reserve. Plunge turnips into salted, boiling water and cook until barely tender. Drain and refresh in cold water. Sauté almonds in 1 tablespoon butter until crisp; reserve. Add the remaining 2 tablespoons butter and the oil to pan. Sauté turnips over high heat until lightly browned. Reduce heat and stir in mustard mixture and almonds. Continue cooking, stirring constantly, until turnips are glazed.

4 to 6 servings.

BAKED SCALLOPED TOMATOES

In the South, sliced tomatoes—usually green but occasionally red—are dipped into cornmeal and fried (nothing is ever sautéed in traditional Southern cooking). These crisp, tangy slices taste delicious, if a bit odd to the uninitiated. Baked Scalloped Tomatoes—either green or red—are kinder to the cook than last-minute frying and equally tasty. Green tomatoes make a dish with a bite, and red tomatoes, a sweeter version. Both seem to call out for charcoal-grilled hamburgers.

4 large green or red tomatoes, peeled

1 teaspoon salt, divided

¼ teaspoon freshly ground, black pepper

½ cup whole, blanched almonds, toasted

5 tablespoons butter, divided

½ cup fresh, white bread crumbs

2 cloves garlic, chopped finely

2 tablespoons chopped, fresh parsley

1 tablespoon chopped, fresh thyme or 1 teaspoon dried thyme

⅔ cup heavy cream

Slice tomatoes ¼-inch thick; season with ½ teaspoon salt and the pepper. Drain on paper towel. Meanwhile, coarsely grind almonds in food processor or blender. Melt 4 tablespoons butter; combine with remaining ½ teaspoon salt, next four ingredients, and ground almonds. Butter a shallow ovenproof dish with the remaining 1 tablespoon butter. Arrange tomato slices in dish. Sprinkle with almond mixture. Evenly drizzle cream over top. For green tomatoes, bake at 475° F. for 30 minutes or until top is lightly browned and tomatoes are just tender. Bake ripe tomatoes at 475° F. for 10 minutes.

6 servings.

SUMMER SQUASH MOCK PASTA

In this recipe, long strands of summer squash resemble spaghetti—at many fewer calories—thus rationalizing the heavy cream and Parmesan. In addition to being a sumptuous accompaniment to meats, this dish easily becomes a whimsical first course or a satisfying, light main dish.

1 cup heavy cream

1 cup chopped, natural almonds

2 tablespoons olive oil, divided

2 yellow zucchini or crookneck squash

2 zucchini

1 tomato, peeled, seeded, diced, and drained

¼ cup freshly grated Parmesan cheese

½ teaspoon salt

¼ teaspoon freshly ground, white pepper

2 tablespoons finely sliced chives

Reduce cream by half; reserve. Sauté almonds in 1 tablespoon oil until crisp; reserve. Cut squash in half crosswise. Next, slice thinly lengthwise. Finally, slice into thin strips to resemble spaghetti strands. Sauté squash in remaining 1 tablespoon oil until just tender. Stir in tomato, cream, cheese, salt, pepper, and almonds. Heat through. Garnish with chives.

6 servings.

SPAGHETTI SQUASH WITH CHEESE

Spaghetti squash, actually an edible gourd though classified a squash, is another vegetable that provides a low-calorie, pasta-like experience. Cooked, this squash organizes itself into long strands—hence, the name. In this recipe, it gets a final sauté with almonds in olive oil, butter, and garlic, then a quick toss with grated Fontina.

1 large spaghetti squash, about 2½ pounds

1 cup chopped, natural almonds

2 tablespoons olive oil

2 tablespoons butter

2 to 3 cloves garlic, chopped finely

½ teaspoon salt

¼ teaspoon freshly ground, white pepper

½ cup grated Fontina cheese

Place whole squash in large baking pan, adding enough water to come two inches up sides. Cover with foil and bake at 350° F. for 45 minutes. Cut squash in half lengthwise; discard seed; with a fork scrape out inside of squash into spaghetti-like strands. Meanwhile, sauté almonds in oil and butter until crisp; stir in garlic. Add spaghetti squash strands and sauté several minutes. Season with salt and pepper. Stir in cheese. 6 servings.

ZUCCHINI WITH ORANGE AND CHIVES

Julienned zucchini with orange and chives delivers a fresh combination of flavors. Try it with pork or duck.

⅔ cup chopped, natural almonds

3 tablespoons butter, divided

1 tablespoon vegetable oil

1½ pounds zucchini, julienned

1 teaspoon salt

¼ cup orange juice

½ teaspoon grated orange peel

1 teaspoon freshly ground, white pepper

¼ cup thinly sliced chives

Sauté almonds in 1 tablespoon butter; reserve. Add the remaining 2 tablespoons butter and oil to pan. Sprinkle zucchini with salt and sauté until barely tender. Deglaze with orange juice. Add orange peel, pepper, and almonds. Remove from heat and stir in chives.

4 to 6 servings.

ALMOND FRIED ZUCCHINI

Fried zucchini should be delicate and crisp on the outside and just tender on the inside. Unfortunately, it rarely is. The secrets to perfectly fried zucchini are a light coating, fresh oil, and the correct temperature. Prepared with these cautions in mind, Almond Fried Zucchini is almost too delicious; it is difficult to stop nibbling. Serve it with a wedge of lemon for a first course — or put a basketful out with drinks.

½ cup flour
Salt
1 clove garlic, chopped finely
2 eggs, lightly beaten
2 cups sliced, natural almonds

¾ pound zucchini, cut in half cross-wise, and sliced ¼-inch thick lengthwise
½ cup milk
Vegetable oil for frying

Combine flour and 2 teaspoons salt; reserve. Mix garlic and beaten eggs; reserve. Lightly crush almonds with hands to break into small pieces. Reserve. Dip each zucchini slice in milk, then in flour, then in egg mixture, and finally in almonds. Fry in hot oil, turning once, until golden brown. Sprinkle lightly with salt.
6 to 8 servings.

SAUTEED ZUCCHINI

Zucchini is readily available, cooks quickly, and marries well with other flavors. The smaller the zucchini, the tastier and the less watery it is. The secret is to cook it quickly and eat it immediately. Here, rosemary, cream, and almonds flavor and enrich a grated zucchini sauté.

¾ cup chopped, natural almonds

3 tablespoons butter

¾ pound zucchini, coarsely grated and squeezed to remove excess liquid

3 tablespoons heavy cream

1½ teaspoons chopped, fresh rosemary or ½ teaspoon dried rosemary

¼ teaspoon salt

¼ teaspoon freshly ground, black pepper

Sauté almonds in 1 tablespoon butter until crisp; reserve. Add remaining 2 tablespoons butter to pan and sauté zucchini 2 to 3 minutes or until just tender. Stir in cream, rosemary, salt, pepper, and almonds. Sauté 1 minute longer over high heat. 4 servings.

MINT PILAF

Mint Pilaf, gutsy with onion, garlic, and beef stock, is a hearty side dish for red meats. The mint naturally and deliciously suggests lamb, but beef fares well with this savory alternative to the ubiquitous potato.

1 cup chopped onion
1 clove garlic, chopped finely
3 tablespoons butter, divided
1 cup long grain rice
2 cups beef stock

3 tablespoons finely chopped, fresh mint or 1 teaspoon dried mint
1 tablespoon fresh lemon juice
½ teaspoon salt
¾ cup blanched, slivered almonds

Sauté onion and garlic in 2 tablespoons butter until soft. Add rice and cook, stirring, 1 minute. Stir in stock, mint, lemon juice, and salt. Bring to a boil. Reduce heat to low, cover, and cook 20 minutes or until all liquid is absorbed. Remove from heat and let stand, covered, 5 minutes. While rice is cooking, sauté almonds in remaining 1 tablespoon butter. Stir into hot, cooked rice.

4 to 6 servings.

ALMOND COCONUT RICE

Rice and almonds are a happy combination. The nuts add crunch to the rice and both combine well with other flavors. Almond Coconut Rice is a lively blend of the sweet and the savory. Diced red bell peppers and a touch of chile powder balance the richness of the almonds and the coconut—all of which beg to be joined by a succulent, crisp-skinned chicken or duck.

1 onion, chopped
1 red bell pepper, diced
2 tablespoons butter
½ teaspoon chile powder
1 cup long grain rice
1¾ cups chicken stock
½ teaspoon salt
¼ teaspoon freshly ground, white pepper
1 cup shredded coconut
⅔ cup sliced, natural almonds, toasted

Sauté onion and red bell pepper in butter until onion is translucent. Stir in chile powder. Add rice and sauté 1 minute longer. Stir in chicken stock, salt, and pepper. Bring to a boil. Reduce heat to low, cover, and cook 20 minutes or until all liquid is absorbed. Remove from heat and let rest 5 minutes. Stir in coconut and almonds.
4 to 6 servings.

SWEET POTATO PUREE

Sweet potato recipes seem to appear only at holiday time and usually involve large amounts of brown sugar, maple syrup or the like. Here is a recipe that deserves year-round attention. It allows the bite of garlic and white pepper to punctuate, rather than overpower, the delicate sweetness of the potato. It is especially good with pork or fowl.

2 large, fresh sweet potatoes
½ cup chopped, natural almonds
6 tablespoons butter, divided
2 cloves garlic, chopped finely
½ teaspoon salt
¼ teaspoon freshly ground, white pepper

Prick sweet potatoes and bake at 350° F. for 1 hour or until potatoes are very soft. Meanwhile, sauté almonds in 1 tablespoon butter until crisp. Stir in garlic and remove from heat; reserve. When potatoes are done, cut in half, scoop out flesh, and purée. Add remaining 5 tablespoons butter to potatoes, a little at a time. Fold in almonds. Season with salt and pepper. Heat over low heat, stirring constantly.
4 to 6 servings.

POTATOES WITH CHEESE AND HERBS

Potatoes seem to beg for embellishment. In this version of a Lyonnaise tradition, a rich combination of cream cheese, crème fraîche, and almonds seasoned with vermouth, fresh herbs, and good olive oil top steamed potatoes. The savory mixture contrasts wonderfully with the sweet blandness of tiny new potatoes. Small portions make an unusual first course. Served in larger quantity with a crisp green salad, a fine, light meal can be made.

12 small or 6 medium, red, new potatoes

6 ounces cream cheese

½ cup *crème fraîche* or sour cream

1 tablespoon dry vermouth

2 teaspoons olive oil

1 small shallot, chopped finely

1 clove garlic, chopped finely

1 tablespoon chopped, fresh parsley

1 tablespoon finely sliced chives

½ cup chopped, natural almonds, toasted

½ teaspoon salt

⅛ teaspoon freshly ground, white pepper

Steam potatoes until just tender. While potatoes are cooking, beat together cream cheese, *crème fraîche,* vermouth, and oil until just blended. Stir in shallots, garlic, parsley, chives, and almonds. Season with salt and pepper; reserve. Quarter hot potatoes and spoon cream cheese mixture into center.

6 servings.

POTATOES AND CAMEMBERT

A sumptuous version of a French peasant dish, this cheese and potato casserole is a rich and savory accompaniment to simple meats. Alternatively, paired with an astringent green salad, it makes a fine and indulgent lunch all by itself.

½ cup chopped, natural almonds
3 tablespoons butter, divided
2 large cloves garlic, chopped finely
2 pounds baking potatoes
2 tablespoons heavy cream
6 medium green onions, finely sliced, including green
¾ teaspoon salt
¼ teaspoon freshly ground, black pepper
8 ounces cold Camembert with rind removed, and diced

Sauté almonds in 1 tablespoon butter until crisp; reserve. Sauté garlic in 1 tablespoon butter until soft; reserve. Cook potatoes in salted, boiling water for about 30 minutes or until tender. Drain and peel. Coarsely mash potatoes. Fold in garlic butter, cream, almonds, green onion, salt, and pepper. Fold in Camembert. Put in an ovenproof dish. Melt remaining 1 tablespoon butter and drizzle over top. Bake at 450° F. for 10 minutes or until top is lightly browned.

6 to 8 servings.

BROILED MUSHROOMS

The success of this dish rests on good quality extra-virgin olive oil. It requires great quantities of crusty bread to sop up the juices.

5 tablespoons olive oil, divided

2 cloves garlic, chopped finely

¼ teaspoon red pepper flakes

1 pound mushrooms, quartered

1 lemon, juiced

½ cup chopped, natural almonds, toasted

½ teaspoon salt

⅛ teaspoon freshly ground, black pepper

Coat the inside of a shallow baking pan with 1 tablespoon olive oil. Mix remaining 4 tablespoons oil with garlic and red pepper flakes; reserve. Toss mushrooms with lemon juice. Add almonds; then toss with oil mixture. Arrange in single layer in baking dish. Season with salt and pepper. Broil 5 to 8 minutes until mushrooms are lightly browned on top.

4 servings.

GRATIN OF BELGIAN ENDIVE

In this dish, the elegant Belgian endive is transformed by heavy cream and Parmesan cheese into a sumptuous gratin. The slight bitterness of the endive, the sweetness of the cream, and the bite of the Parmesan all combine to make a luxurious accompaniment to simple roasts or will make a fine first course.

3 tablespoons butter

6 medium Belgian endive (about 2 pounds)

½ teaspoon salt

¼ teaspoon freshly ground, white pepper

½ cup freshly grated, Parmesan cheese

⅓ cup bread crumbs

⅔ cup chopped, natural almonds, toasted

2 tablespoons chopped, fresh parsley

¾ cup heavy cream

1 lemon for garnish

Generously butter a shallow baking pan with the 3 tablespoons butter; reserve. Trim and core endive; cut in half lengthwise. Place cut-side down in pan. Season with salt and pepper. Mix cheese, bread crumbs, almonds, and parsley; sprinkle over endive. Bake at 450° F. for 5 minutes. Reduce heat to 375° F. and continue baking 30 minutes. Pour cream over and bake 10 minutes longer. Serve with lemon wedges. 4 servings.

GRATIN OF CAULIFLOWER

Cauliflower, a relative of the cabbage, has suffered many of the same indignities in the kitchen. Usually overcooked and watery, with a distinctive off-odor, it does not win friends easily. Treated properly, cauliflower is tasty and interesting whether raw or cooked. This rich gratin could convert die-hard cauliflower haters. Gratin of Cauliflower can be prepared ahead up to the final ten-minute baking, which makes it appealing to the cook with guests. A seemly accompaniment to simple meats, it is also a fine first course.

5 tablespoons butter, divided

2 tablespoons flour

1 cup milk

1 onion, quartered

1 bay leaf

2 whole cloves

¼ teaspoon salt

⅛ teaspoon freshly ground, white pepper

1 large head cauliflower, about 2 pounds

2 tablespoons lemon juice, divided

⅔ cup blanched, slivered almonds

1 clove garlic, chopped finely

¼ cup fresh, white bread crumbs

½ cup freshly grated Parmesan cheese

Melt 1 tablespoon butter in heavy saucepan; add flour and stir to smooth paste. Cook over low heat, stirring constantly, for 10 minutes. Add milk, stirring to prevent lumps. Add onion, bay leaf, cloves, salt, and pepper. Cook 10 to 15 minutes over low heat; strain and reserve. Trim cauliflower and break into flowerets. Plunge into salted, boiling water to which 1 tablespoon lemon juice has been added. Cook over medium heat, uncovered, 4 to 5 minutes or until barely tender; drain and reserve. Sauté almonds in remaining 4 tablespoons butter until they begin to color. Add garlic and remove from heat. Add remaining 1 tablespoon lemon juice; reserve. Arrange cauliflower in a gratin dish; pour reserved sauce over cauliflower. Mix bread crumbs and cheese and sprinkle over sauce. Top with almond mixture. Bake at 500° F. for about 10 minutes until lightly browned.

6 servings.

RUM CARROTS

Carrots seem to lack a certain glamour, perhaps because we have been told from childhood that they are good for us. While Rum Carrots are still healthy fare and do not require a bank loan to execute, this preparation of smartly julienned carrots, combined with the lively flavors of rum, ginger, and lime and the crunch of almonds, tastes quite wonderful. This dish clearly could be invited to a dinner party.

½ cup blanched, slivered almonds

5 tablespoons butter, divided

¾ pound carrots, julienned

2 tablespoons chopped shallots

1 teaspoon grated, fresh ginger or ¼ teaspoon powdered ginger

3 tablespoons light rum

1 tablespoon lime juice

½ teaspoon sugar

½ teaspoon salt

Pinch freshly ground, white pepper

Sauté almonds in 1 tablespoon butter until golden; reserve. Sauté carrots in 3 tablespoons butter, stirring occasionally, 3 to 4 minutes or until just tender. Add remaining 1 tablespoon butter to pan. Add shallots and ginger; cook 1 minute. Add rum. Ignite by touching the edge of the pan with the flame of a match. Allow to burn until flame dies out. Always use caution when flaming. Remove from heat and stir in almonds and last four ingredients.

4 to 6 servings.

SAUTEED GREEN CABBAGE

Green cabbage is an underrated vegetable, which is a shame. Raw, it adds tang and texture to salads, and properly cooked, it gives good account of itself. In this recipe, once blanched, the cabbage is sautéed briefly in a bit of butter and oil, then finished with sour cream and almonds. Try it with sausage, pork, duck or even goose.

¾ cup chopped, natural almonds

2 tablespoons vegetable oil, divided

1 small head green cabbage, about 1 pound

1 tablespoon butter

½ cup sour cream

½ teaspoon freshly ground, white pepper

½ teaspoon salt

⅛ teaspoon freshly grated nutmeg

1 teaspoon lemon juice

Sauté almonds in 1 tablespoon oil until crisp; reserve. Slice cabbage 1-inch thick. Plunge into salted, boiling water and cook until just tender; drain. Sauté cabbage in remaining 1 tablespoon oil and the butter 2 to 3 minutes. Stir in sour cream, pepper, salt, nutmeg, lemon juice, and almonds.

6 servings.

RED BELL PEPPER SAUTE

This red bell pepper sauté is a delicious and unusual accompaniment to meats. The sweet bite of the pepper with the pungency of garlic and cilantro contrasts especially well with the richness of lamb. Alternatively, toss it with hot, buttered pasta.

½ cup chopped, natural almonds

2 tablespoons vegetable oil, divided

2 red bell peppers, cut into 1-inch squares

1 tablespoon sugar

1 teaspoon lemon juice

1 teaspoon salt

¼ teaspoon red pepper flakes

1 clove garlic, chopped finely

1 anchovy, chopped finely

1 tablespoon finely chopped, fresh cilantro

Sauté almonds in 1 tablespoon oil until crisp; reserve. Add remaining 1 tablespoon oil to pan and sauté bell pepper until just tender. Stir in sugar and cook, stirring constantly, until melted. Stir in lemon juice, salt, red pepper flakes, garlic, anchovy, cilantro, and almonds.

4 to 6 servings.

GREEN BEANS WITH ALMONDS AND SHERRY

It would seem there is little new to say about green beans and almonds. However, the addition of sage and dry sherry creates an elegant and complex note in this dish.

½ pound green beans, sliced into 1-inch pieces

½ cup blanched, slivered almonds

2 tablespoons butter, divided

2 teaspoons vegetable oil

1 teaspoon chopped, fresh sage or ¼ teaspoon dried, leaf sage

¼ teaspoon salt

¼ cup dry sherry

Plunge green beans into salted, boiling water and cook until barely tender. Beans should be crisp and bright green. Drain and refresh in cold water. Sauté green beans and almonds in 1 tablespoon butter mixed with oil until almonds are golden, about 3 to 5 minutes. Stir in sage and salt. Remove to a warm plate. Add sherry to pan and reduce over high heat to a syrupy consistency. Stir in remaining 1 tablespoon butter; drizzle over beans and almonds.

4 servings.

ASPARAGUS SAUTE

Asparagus takes on an Oriental theme in this recipe. Thin slices of garlic, lemon juice, and a touch of sweetness punctuate the fresh flavor of a springtime favorite. In this company, the garlic is surprisingly well-mannered.

1½ pounds asparagus, trimmed and sliced diagonally into 1½-inch pieces

4 cloves garlic, sliced thinly lengthwise

2 tablespoons butter

½ cup sliced, natural almonds

2 tablespoons lemon juice

1 tablespoon sugar

½ teaspoon salt

⅛ teaspoon freshly ground, black pepper

Plunge asparagus into salted, boiling water and cook until just tender. Asparagus should be crisp and bright green. Drain and refresh in cold water. Sauté garlic in butter for 1 minute. Add almonds and sauté 1 minute. Add lemon juice and sugar; cook, stirring, until sugar melts and begins to caramelize. Add asparagus and heat, stirring to coat with sauce. Season with salt and pepper.

4 servings.

ASPARAGUS BAKED WITH PARMESAN AND ALMONDS

Asparagus, with its delicate herbaceous flavor, is almost universally popular. It requires little more than a touch of butter to be enjoyed. But, after the first spring excitement has subsided and simplicity has lost some attraction, one wants to embellish. Parmesan cheese, almonds, and asparagus combine quite compatibly in this sumptuous gratin that can be prepared ahead of time. It's a fine side dish, but almost better as a first course or a light luncheon dish, where it gets full attention.

⅓ cup blanched, whole almonds, toasted

⅓ cup freshly grated Parmesan cheese

¼ teaspoon salt

1½ pounds asparagus, trimmed

4 tablespoons butter, divided

Lemon wedges for garnish

Coarsely grind almonds in food processor or blender. Mix with Parmesan cheese and salt; reserve. Plunge asparagus into salted, boiling water and cook until barely tender. Asparagus should be crisp and bright green. Drain and refresh in cold water. Butter a shallow, ovenproof dish with 1 tablespoon butter. Arrange asparagus in dish. Top with almond mixture. Dot with remaining 3 tablespoons butter. Bake at 450° F. for about 20 minutes or until top is golden brown. Let rest 5 minutes. Serve with lemon wedges.

4 to 6 servings.

ARTICHOKE SAUTE WITH MUSTARD AND CHIVES

Many people outside California think of artichokes as an exotic first course, usually steamed whole and served with a sauce for dipping — or they are familiar with artichoke hearts in small jars, marinated and ready to toss into a salad. In fact, artichokes are a wonderfully versatile vegetable, useful in soups, appetizers, main dishes, and salads. This artichoke sauté, seasoned with mustard, chives, and lemon juice, is a piquant accompaniment to simple chicken, veal, and fish dishes.

⅔ cup chopped, natural almonds

3 tablespoons olive oil, divided

24 tiny, fresh artichokes (2 packages, 9 ounces each, frozen artichoke hearts may be substituted)

¼ cup butter

2 tablespoons Dijon mustard

1 tablespoon lemon juice

¼ cup chopped, fresh parsley

2 tablespoons finely sliced chives

½ teaspoon salt

¼ teaspoon freshly ground, white pepper

Sauté almonds in 1 tablespoon oil until crisp; reserve. For fresh artichokes, trim stem, remove tough outer leaves, and top of artichoke. Plunge into salted, boiling water for 3 to 4 minutes or until just tender. Drain. Thinly slice artichokes lengthwise. (Defrost frozen artichoke hearts and use just as they come in the package.) Sauté artichokes in butter, 3 to 4 minutes. Add mustard and lemon juice, and sauté 1 minute longer. Toss with almonds, parsley, chives, and remaining 2 tablespoons oil. Season with salt and pepper.

6 servings.

CHICKEN BREASTS WITH ALMONDS AND GREEN GRAPES

Chicken has a lot going for it. It's inexpensive, low in fat and calories, versatile, and delicious. The very best are grain fed and are becoming increasingly available. They cost a bit more but the taste is worth it. It's wise to avoid freezing chicken—except for bones and the odd scrap destined for the stockpot—because freezing does noticeably affect texture and flavor. One final note of caution: the greatest danger in preparing chicken is overcooking. In this recipe, delicately poached chicken breasts are blanketed with a sauce of reduced cream and slightly sweet sherry. The addition of fresh, green grapes balances the richness. Serve with fine egg noodles tossed with butter and freshly ground white pepper.

2 whole chicken breasts, skinned, boned, and cut in half
⅔ cup sliced, natural almonds
1 tablespoon butter
½ small onion, chopped finely
1 clove garlic, chopped finely
1½ cups chicken stock
1 cup heavy cream
¼ cup amontillado (medium) sherry
⅔ cup seedless green grapes, cut in half lengthwise
¼ teaspoon salt
¼ teaspoon freshly ground, white pepper
2 pinches freshly grated nutmeg

Lightly flatten chicken breasts; reserve. Sauté almonds in butter until golden; remove with slotted spoon and reserve. In butter remaining in pan, sauté onion until translucent; add garlic, then chicken stock. Reduce liquid to about ½ cup; strain and reserve. In large skillet, reduce cream to ¾ cup; strain and return to skillet. Gradually add chicken stock mixture to cream. Place chicken breasts on top; cover, and simmer 5 to 7 minutes or until tender. Remove chicken and keep warm. Reduce sauce until it thickens and lightly coats the back of a spoon, 15 to 20 minutes. Add sherry, grapes, salt, pepper, and nutmeg; simmer 3 minutes longer. Stir in almonds. Pour sauce over chicken.

4 servings.

CHICKEN BREASTS STUFFED WITH GOAT CHEESE

This rich chicken dish takes advantage of the increasing popularity of goat cheese and is well-suited for a dinner party. It may be assembled in advance and held in the refrigerator. Allow a few minutes extra in the oven to compensate for the chilling.

2 whole chicken breasts, skinned, boned, and cut in half

1¼ cups chopped, natural almonds, toasted, divided

6 ounces goat cheese

1 cup + 2 tablespoons butter, divided

2 shallots, chopped finely

⅔ cup dry white wine

3 tablespoons lemon juice

Lightly flatten chicken breasts; reserve. Combine ¾ cup almonds and goat cheese; form into log ½-inch in diameter and cut into 4 pieces. Lay chicken breasts upside down and place one piece cheese mixture on each. Fold sides lengthwise into center, sealing edges firmly. Cut four pieces of aluminum foil 5 x 11-inches. Place one breast, top side up, in the center of each piece of foil. Fold sides up around chicken, twisting both ends to tighten and form a boat. Melt 1 tablespoon butter and paint the top of each breast. Bake at 425° F. for 8 to 10 minutes; remove from oven and take off foil. Meanwhile, sauté shallots in 1 tablespoon butter until translucent. Add wine and lemon juice; reduce until about 2 tablespoons liquid remain. Over very low heat, whisk in remaining 1 cup butter, a little at a time; strain. (Sauce may be kept warm over hot water until ready.) Just before serving, add remaining ½ cup almonds to sauce. Pour over chicken breasts.

4 servings.

CHICKEN BREASTS SAUTEED WITH CORIANDER AND ORANGE

Sautéing in butter is a toothsome method of cooking chicken breasts that produces delicately textured, juicy meat. Prepared in this manner, chicken should be served as soon as the sauce is ready, to preserve its best character. In this version, the compatible flavors of coriander and orange season a vermouth-based sauce.

2 whole chicken breasts, skinned, boned, and cut in half

5 tablespoons butter, divided

1 tablespoon finely chopped shallots

2 cloves garlic, chopped finely

1 teaspoon whole coriander seeds, crushed

⅔ cup orange juice

1 cup dry vermouth

¼ teaspoon salt

½ cup sliced, natural almonds, toasted

Sauté chicken in 3 tablespoons butter over medium heat, turning occasionally, 10 to 15 minutes or until tender. Remove and keep warm. To butter remaining in pan, add shallots, garlic, and coriander seeds; cook 2 to 3 minutes. Add orange juice and reduce to a syrupy consistency. Add vermouth and reduce by half. Add salt and remaining 2 tablespoons butter. Strain sauce. Stir in almonds and pour over chicken. 4 servings.

CHICKEN BREASTS WITH ORANGE AND MUSTARD

This recipe is ideal when one has to produce an elegant, little meal quickly—especially if the butcher bones, skins, and splits the chicken breasts. Orange marmalade, coarse-grained mustard, and almonds, when combined, taste wonderful, and the cream adds a luxurious note. Rice cooked in chicken stock and buttered asparagus or green beans easily complete the plate.

⅔ cup sliced, natural almonds
3 tablespoons butter, divided
3 whole chicken breasts, skinned, boned, and cut in half
Salt
Freshly ground, white pepper

1½ cups heavy cream
4 teaspoons coarse-grained mustard
2 tablespoons orange marmalade
⅛ teaspoon cayenne

Sauté almonds in 1 tablespoon butter until crisp; reserve. Season chicken with salt and white pepper. In remaining 2 tablespoons butter, sauté chicken over medium-high heat for 30 seconds on each side. Add cream, mustard, marmalade, ½ teaspoon salt, ¼ teaspoon freshly ground, white pepper, and cayenne. Reduce over medium heat until sauce thickens and coats the back of a spoon, and chicken is tender, approximately 10 minutes. Stir in almonds.

6 servings.

ALMOND CHICKEN PAPRIKA

Almond Chicken Paprika is a version of the classic, Hungarian dish. Here crunchy ground almonds deliciously coat the chicken and protect its juiciness. The traditional flavors of paprika and sour cream in the sauce marry perfectly with the nuttiness of the almonds. The sauce can be cooked ahead, and the chicken prepared up to the final baking and held in the refrigerator. The rich sauce begs for noodles or tiny dumplings.

1 cup whole, natural almonds, toasted
2 whole chicken breasts, skinned, boned, and cut in half
Salt
Freshly ground, white pepper
8 tablespoons butter, divided
2 teaspoons Dijon mustard
2½ tablespoons paprika, divided
Flour
⅔ cup chopped onion
Pinch cayenne
1 cup chicken stock
½ cup sour cream

Coarsely chop almonds; reserve. Lightly flatten chicken breasts. Season with salt and pepper. Melt 6 tablespoons of butter. Whisk in mustard and 1 tablespoon paprika. Dredge chicken in flour, then in mustard mixture. Coat with almonds. Place on buttered baking sheet. Bake at 450° F. for 10 to 15 minutes or until chicken is just firm. Meanwhile, melt remaining 2 tablespoons butter in saucepan. Add onion and sauté until translucent. Stir in remaining 1½ tablespoons paprika, 1 tablespoon flour, ½ teaspoon salt, and cayenne. Cook 1 minute. Stir in chicken stock; simmer 5 minutes. Whisk in sour cream; heat through. *Do not boil.* Divide sauce among four serving plates and top each with a chicken breast.
4 servings.

ALMOND CHICKEN DIJON

Here, almond-crusted chicken breasts are prepared à la diable. Like the previous recipe, they can be prepared in advance up to the final baking. They are equally at home at the dining room table or on a picnic.

¾ cup whole, natural almonds, toasted

2 tablespoons flour

2 whole chicken breasts, skinned, boned, and cut in half

Salt

Freshly ground, white pepper

2 tablespoons melted butter

1 teaspoon Worcestershire sauce

2 dashes hot pepper sauce

¼ cup Dijon mustard

Finely grind almonds in food processor or blender. Combine flour and almonds; reserve. Season chicken with salt and pepper. Stir butter, Worcestershire sauce, and hot pepper sauce into mustard. Heavily coat each chicken breast with mustard mixture. Roll in ground almonds, coating chicken thoroughly. Bake on buttered cookie sheet at 500° F. for 8 to 10 minutes or until chicken is just firm.

4 servings.

CHICKEN RAGOUT WITH CHILES, TORTILLAS, AND GOAT CHEESE

This pungent mixture of chicken, green chiles, goat cheese, and almonds has its origins in regional Mexican cuisine. Because the ingredients are already cut into manageable bits, it's a fine buffet dish. Serve it with a mélange of sautéed, summer squashes and plain rice pilaf.

1 cup sliced, natural almonds

6 tablespoons vegetable oil, divided

6 corn tortillas

2 whole chicken breasts, skinned, boned, and cut in half

1 cup chicken stock

1 onion, chopped

1 red bell pepper, julienned

1 can (7 ounces) whole green chiles, cut crosswise into ¼-inch strips

1½ teaspoons ground cumin

1 cup heavy cream

½ pound goat cheese

1 tablespoon lime juice

1 teaspoon salt

Sauté almonds in 1 tablespoon oil until golden; reserve. Heat 4 tablespoons oil and soften tortillas, one at a time for about 30 seconds. Drain. Cut tortillas into ½-inch strips and reserve. Poach chicken breasts, covered, in barely simmering chicken stock, about 10 minutes or until just tender. Reserve chicken stock; slice chicken into strips. In large skillet, sauté onion and bell pepper in the remaining 1 tablespoon oil, until onions are translucent. Add chiles and cumin and sauté 1 minute longer. Stir in reserved stock and cream; simmer 2 to 3 minutes. Add chicken. Stir in goat cheese; *do not boil.* Add lime juice and salt. Fold in tortilla strips and almonds.

4 servings.

BAKED CURRIED CHICKEN

Here is baked chicken redolent of curry spices and treated to a final coating of crisp ground almonds. Innocent-looking pieces of crusty chicken surprise and delight upon first bite, with the warmth of the aromatic seasonings.

1⅔ cups blanched, whole almonds, toasted

½ cup plain yogurt

¼ cup vegetable oil

2 tablespoons lime juice

¼ cup honey

2 tablespoons curry powder

4 cloves garlic, chopped finely

1 teaspoon grated, fresh ginger or ¼ teaspoon powdered ginger

1½ teaspoons salt

8 chicken thighs, skinned

Coarsely grind almonds in food processor or blender; reserve. Combine next eight ingredients. Using half of the yogurt mixture, coat chicken. Place chicken on rack in pan and bake at 550° F. for 15 minutes. Remove and coat with remaining yogurt mixture. Roll chicken pieces in ground almonds, pressing almonds into chicken. Return to oven and continue cooking 10 to 15 minutes or until tender.
4 servings.

CORNBREAD AND SAUSAGE STUFFED CHICKEN

Stuffing poultry between the skin and the flesh produces well-flavored, juicy, tender meat and delicious, moist stuffing. The chicken roasts more quickly and is easier to carve when its backbone is removed and its breastbone flattened than when prepared conventionally. In this recipe, a mixture of cornbread, spicy sausage, and aromatic vegetables, bound together by heavy cream, provides a robust contrast to the flavor of the meat.

¾ cup chopped, natural almonds
1 tablespoon butter
2 hot Italian sausage links
1 small red onion, finely diced
2 cloves garlic, chopped finely
1 small stalk celery, finely diced

3 cups crumbled cornbread
½ cup heavy cream
½ teaspoon salt
¼ teaspoon freshly ground, black pepper
1 chicken, about 3½ pounds

Sauté almonds in butter until crisp; remove and reserve. Remove casing from sausage and sauté, until brown and crumbly. Add onion, garlic, and celery; sauté until translucent. Remove from heat. Add cornbread, cream, and almonds and mix thoroughly. Season with salt and pepper. Cut chicken along each side of the backbone to remove bone. (Reserve neck, giblets, and liver for other use.) With heel of hand, smash the breastbone to flatten. Carefully run hand between flesh and skin on both sides of the breastbone, loosening skin on breasts, thighs, and drumsticks. Stuff cornbread mixture between skin and flesh. Cut a slit in the loose skin on each side of the breastbone end. With drumsticks turned in toward body, insert tips into slits. Bake at 475° F. for 10 minutes. Reduce heat to 350° F. and continue baking 30 minutes or until juice runs clear when thigh is pierced. Let rest 10 minutes.
4 servings.

ROAST CHICKEN WITH HONEY, BLACK PEPPER, AND ALMONDS

The flavors of honey and black pepper provide the perfect point and counterpoint to this succulent, roasted chicken. Like the previous recipe, the chicken is stuffed beneath the skin, but this time with a compound butter, which perfumes the meat and keeps it moist. Finally, the deep glaze of a classically prepared, brown poultry sauce, dotted with sliced almonds, blankets the crisp skin. Oven-roasted potatoes or real, hand-whipped, garlic-scented mashed potatoes go deliciously alongside.

4 tablespoons butter, divided

3½ tablespoons honey, divided

1¾ teaspoons freshly ground, black pepper, divided

1 whole chicken, about 3½ pounds

1 tablespoon vegetable oil

1 carrot, diced

1 stalk celery, diced

½ onion, diced

½ cup dry white wine

3½ cups chicken stock

Salt

½ cup sliced, natural almonds, toasted

Mix 2 tablespoons butter, 2 tablespoons honey, and 1 teaspoon pepper; reserve. Cut chicken along each side of backbone to remove bone; reserve with neck and giblets. (Reserve liver for another use.) Remove wings at second joint; reserve. With heel of hand, smash the breastbone to flatten. Carefully run hand between flesh and skin on both sides of the breastbone, loosening skin on breasts, thighs, and drumsticks. Thoroughly rub butter mixture between skin and flesh. Cut a slit in the loose skin on each side of the breastbone end. With drumsticks turned in toward body, insert tips into slits. Set aside. Chop wings, backbone, neck, and giblets into small pieces; brown in oil. Add carrots, celery, and onion and sauté until brown. Add wine and stock. Simmer, skimming off fat, until approximately 1½ cups liquid remain. Meanwhile, season chicken with salt. Bake at 425° F. for 10 minutes. Reduce heat to 375° F. and bake 25 minutes longer or until juice runs clear when thigh is pierced. Let rest 10 minutes. When stock is done, strain and reserve. Melt 1 tablespoon butter. Add remaining 1½ tablespoons honey and remaining ¾ teaspoon pepper. Slowly add hot stock; simmer 1 minute. Remove from heat and swirl in remaining 1 tablespoon butter. Add almonds. Pour sauce over chicken.
4 servings.

CALIFORNIA CHICKEN MOLE

In this version of a Mexican classic, ground almonds thicken and enrich the spicy sauce. Chocolate may seem an odd addition to those not familiar with this dish, but it contributes to the depth of flavor and mahogany color of the sauce. Plain, steamed rice is the perfect foil for this rich and pungent sauce.

¾ cup blanched, slivered almonds

3 tablespoons vegetable oil, divided

¼ teaspoon ground cumin

⅛ teaspoon cinnamon

⅛ teaspoon ground cloves

⅛ teaspoon coriander

Freshly ground, black pepper

¼ cup fresh, white bread crumbs

4 canned jalapeño peppers, stems and seeds removed

2 cloves garlic, chopped finely

1½ cups chicken stock

1 ounce semisweet chocolate, chopped

Salt

1 chicken, about 3½ pounds, cut up

Sauté almonds in 1 tablespoon oil until golden. Remove ¼ cup almonds; reserve. Add next four ingredients and ⅛ teaspoon pepper to remaining ½ cup almonds; sauté 1 minute. Stir in bread crumbs, jalapeño peppers, garlic, chicken stock, chocolate, and ½ teaspoon salt; simmer 5 minutes. Purée and reserve. Season chicken with salt and pepper and brown in remaining 2 tablespoons oil. Pour off fat from pan. Add sauce, cover, and simmer 15 to 20 minutes, turning once, until chicken is tender. (Add additional stock if sauce gets too thick.) Garnish with remaining ¼ cup almonds. 4 servings.

ALMOND CHICKEN WITH ONION

Fricassees are not harmed by rebeating, and thus are perfect for advance preparation; also, the recipes are easily doubled for a second meal. Lots of thinly sliced onions caramelized to a golden brown give this fricassee a rich color and dense flavor. Cilantro and sherry add intriguing background notes.

1 chicken, about 3½ pounds, cut up

3 tablespoons vegetable oil

2 medium onions, cut in half and sliced thinly

3 cloves garlic, chopped finely

2 tablespoons chopped, fresh cilantro

1 tablespoon chopped, fresh thyme or 1 teaspoon dried thyme

½ teaspoon salt

¼ teaspoon freshly grated nutmeg

1 cup chicken stock

⅓ cup amontillado (medium) sherry

1 teaspoon lemon juice

¾ cup + 1 tablespoon sliced, natural almonds, toasted, divided

Brown chicken in oil. Remove and reserve. Pour off all but 1 tablespoon oil. Add onion and garlic; cook over low heat, stirring, until golden brown. Stir in cilantro, thyme, salt, and nutmeg. Add chicken and chicken stock. Cover and cook 15 to 20 minutes or until chicken is tender. Remove chicken and keep warm. Stir in sherry and reduce sauce 5 minutes or until sauce coats the back of a spoon. Add lemon juice and ¾ cup almonds. Pour sauce over chicken and sprinkle with remaining 1 tablespoon almonds.

4 servings.

CHICKEN WITH BRANDY AND CREAM

Brandy or other spirits add a subtle complexity to sauces—especially those made without the benefit of a long-simmered stock. The alcohol burns off neatly when flamed.

1 chicken, about 3½ pounds, cut up

Salt

Freshly ground, white pepper

Flour

2 tablespoons butter

1 tablespoon vegetable oil

¼ cup chopped shallots

2 cloves garlic, chopped finely

⅓ cup brandy

1½ cups heavy cream

1 teaspoon lemon juice

¾ cup sliced, natural almonds, toasted

Season chicken with salt and pepper. Dredge in flour; pat off excess. Brown chicken in butter and oil; remove and reserve. Drain all but 1 tablespoon fat from pan. Add shallots and garlic; sauté until shallots are translucent. Add brandy and ignite by touching the edge of the pan with the flame of a match. Allow to burn until flame dies out. Always use caution when flaming. Add cream and return chicken to pan; cook, covered, over medium heat, about 10 to 15 minutes. Remove cover and cook 5 minutes longer or until chicken is tender. Transfer chicken to a warm platter; stir ½ teaspoon salt, lemon juice, and almonds into sauce in pan. Pour over chicken. 4 servings.

BAKED CHICKEN WITH ALMONDS, MUSHROOMS, AND OLIVES

Here is an intriguing one-dish chicken and rice mélange with Spanish origins. Cooked by the same technique as the classic <u>paella</u>, the rice has an excellent texture and absorbs delicious flavors from the other ingredients.

1 cup blanched, slivered almonds
½ cup olive oil
Salt
½ pound mushrooms, quartered
1 chicken, about 3½ pounds, cut up
Freshly ground, black pepper
1 onion, chopped
2 cloves garlic, chopped finely

1 tablespoon chopped, fresh oregano
   or 1 teaspoon dried oregano
1 cup long grain rice
2 cups chicken stock
½ cup dry white wine
⅛ teaspoon cayenne
½ cup chopped, pimiento-stuffed olives
Lemon wedges for garnish

Sauté almonds in oil until golden. Remove with slotted spoon and sprinkle with salt; reserve. In oil remaining in skillet, sauté mushrooms over high heat, 2 to 3 minutes. Remove with slotted spoon; reserve. Season chicken with salt and pepper. In oil remaining in skillet, sauté chicken pieces until brown; remove with slotted spoon and reserve. Add onion, garlic, and oregano to skillet and sauté until onion is translucent. Add rice and sauté 1 minute. Add chicken stock, white wine, ½ teaspoon salt, and cayenne; bring to a boil. Bake, uncovered, at 400° F. on lowest rack in oven for 15 minutes. Arrange chicken pieces on top. Continue baking 10 to 15 minutes or until all liquid is absorbed and chicken is tender. Turn off heat and sprinkle top with almonds, mushrooms, and olives (do not stir). Let stand in oven 5 minutes. Garnish with lemon wedges.

4 servings.

CHICKEN AND RICE WITH BLACK OLIVES, FENNEL, AND ORANGE

The wonderful flavors of the Mediterranean—tomato, black olives, fennel, and orange—delight the palate in this easy yet festive dish. The ingredients become perfumed with aromas reminiscent of the south of France. Copious amounts of a dry rosé are in order.

1 chicken, about 3½ pounds, cut up
1 lemon, juiced
1 tablespoon chopped, fresh thyme or 1 teaspoon dried thyme
1 cup blanched, slivered almonds
4 tablespoons olive oil, divided
Salt
Freshly ground, black pepper
2 cups chopped onion

2 cloves garlic, chopped finely
1 cup long grain rice
2 tomatoes, peeled, seeded, and diced
½ cup dry white wine
1½ cups chicken stock
1 teaspoon fennel seeds, crushed
½ teaspoon grated orange peel
¾ cup black Nicoise olives or other imported, black olives

Rub chicken pieces with lemon juice and thyme. Marinate at room temperature for 30 minutes. Sauté almonds in 1 tablespoon oil; reserve. Season chicken with salt and pepper. Sauté chicken in remaining 3 tablespoons oil until browned. Remove with slotted spoon and reserve. In oil remaining in pan, sauté onion and garlic for 2 to 3 minutes or until translucent. Add rice and sauté 1 minute. Add tomatoes, then white wine. Add chicken stock, fennel seeds, orange peel, and 1½ teaspoons salt; bring to a boil. Bake, uncovered, at 400° F. on lowest rack in oven for 15 minutes. Add olives, almonds, and chicken pieces. Continue baking 10 to 15 minutes or until all liquid is absorbed. Remove from oven and let stand 5 minutes.

4 servings.

CHICKEN AND ROASTED PEPPERS

This dish pairs strips of sweet, red bell pepper with pieces of chicken, all infused with the delicate flavor of amontillado sherry. Crisp, sautéed potatoes with a sprinkling of fresh herbs would complement this nicely.

¾ cup chopped, natural almonds

5 tablespoons olive oil, divided

4 large, red bell peppers

1 chicken, about 3½ pounds, cut up

Salt

Freshly ground, white pepper

2 cloves garlic, chopped finely

½ cup amontillado (medium) sherry

Sauté almonds in 1 tablespoon oil until crisp; reserve. Roast peppers under broiler or on a long fork held over a gas flame, turning occasionally, until skins are blackened. Place in paper bag 10 minutes to soften skin. Under cold running water, scrape blackened skin from peppers. Remove stem and seeds. Cut peppers into 1½ x ½-inch strips; reserve. Season chicken with salt and pepper. Sauté chicken in 2 tablespoons oil until golden brown; remove and reserve. Add remaining 2 tablespoons oil and sauté pepper strips 2 minutes. Add garlic, then deglaze with sherry. Return chicken to pan; cook, covered, over low heat 10 to 15 minutes or until tender. Stir in almonds. 4 servings.

Tart, fresh plums are a wonderful contrast to succulent pieces of chicken sautéed in fruity olive oil. In this recipe the thick, puréed sauce is enlivened with aromatic spices, onion, and garlic. Rice cooked in chicken broth is a perfect accompaniment.

1 cup blanched, slivered almonds

5 tablespoons olive oil, divided

6 fresh purple plums, about 1½ pounds, pitted and cut into chunks

1½ tablespoons grated, fresh ginger or ½ teaspoon powdered ginger

½ teaspoon cinnamon

¼ teaspoon ground cloves

1 chicken, about 3½ pounds, cut up and skinned

2 onions, chopped

2 cloves garlic, chopped finely

⅛ teaspoon cayenne

2 tablespoons honey

1 teaspoon salt

3 tablespoons butter

Sauté almonds in 1 tablespoon oil until golden; reserve. In food processor or blender, purée plums with ginger, cinnamon, and cloves; reserve. Sauté chicken in 3 tablespoons oil until browned, about 5 minutes; remove and reserve. Add remaining 1 tablespoon oil to pan and sauté onions until translucent. Add garlic, cayenne, plum mixture, honey, and salt. Place chicken pieces on top. Cook, uncovered, over medium-high heat, 5 minutes on each side or until tender. Remove chicken to serving platter and keep warm. Stir butter and almonds into sauce. Spoon sauce over chicken.
4 servings.

CHICKEN LIVERS AND ALMONDS MADEIRA

Here's a dish comfortably at home at brunch, lunch or dinner. Truly fresh chicken livers sautéed quickly to perfection make fine eating. An outside of butter, crusty brown envelops succulent, slightly pink flesh. In this recipe, slivered almonds are the perfect textural contrast. A dash of Madeira and bits of tomato lighten this dish. Steamed rice is a perfect accompaniment.

1 pound chicken livers, cleaned

Flour seasoned with salt and freshly ground, black pepper

4 tablespoons butter, divided

1 tablespoon vegetable oil

¼ cup finely chopped shallots

¼ pound mushrooms, sliced

½ cup blanched, slivered almonds, toasted

¼ cup Madeira wine

1 small tomato, peeled, seeded, and chopped finely

Lightly dredge chicken livers in seasoned flour; shake to remove excess. Brown over medium heat in 2 tablespoons butter and 1 tablespoon oil, turning once. Remove livers to plate and reserve. Add remaining 2 tablespoons butter to pan and sauté shallots until translucent. Add mushrooms and sauté 2 to 3 minutes or until just done. Add almonds. Deglaze pan with Madeira. Add tomato. Reduce over high heat to syrupy consistency. Return livers to pan and heat through.

4 servings.

LEMON MARMALADE CHICKEN

The delicate flavor of breast of chicken blooms in this pungent lemon sauce. Dijon mustard, garlic, and red pepper flakes are perfect foils for the sweetness of the lemon marmalade. Serve with steamed rice and fresh asparagus for a quick, elegant dinner.

½ cup lemon juice (about 2 to 3 lemons)

3 tablespoons Dijon mustard

2 cloves garlic, chopped finely

¼ teaspoon freshly ground, white pepper

½ cup + 2 tablespoons olive oil, divided

3 whole chicken breasts, skinned, boned, and cut in half

1 cup sliced, natural almonds

2 cups chicken stock

1 teaspoon cornstarch dissolved in 1 tablespoon water

2 tablespoons lemon marmalade (orange marmalade may be substituted)

2 tablespoons butter, cut into bits

2 tablespoons chopped, fresh parsley

¼ teaspoon red pepper flakes

Lemon slices for garnish

Combine first 4 ingredients. Whisk in ½ cup oil. Place chicken in a shallow dish just large enough to hold breasts in one layer. Pour on marinade, turning chicken once to coat evenly. Marinate for 1 hour at room temperature or several hours in the refrigerator. When ready to prepare, sauté almonds in 1 tablespoon oil until golden. Remove and reserve. Wipe out pan. Drain chicken, reserving marinade. Sauté chicken over high heat in remaining 1 tablespoon oil, 2 to 3 minutes on each side, until golden. Remove chicken and reserve. Strain marinade into pan. Add chicken stock and cornstarch mixture. Cook over high heat, stirring occasionally, until sauce thickens and coats the back of a spoon, about 5 minutes. Stir in marmalade. Return chicken to pan and heat through. Remove from heat and place chicken on serving platter. Stir butter, parsley, and red pepper flakes into sauce. Add almonds. Pour sauce over chicken. Garnish with lemon slices.

6 servings.

DUCK WITH ORANGE AND GREEN PEPPERCORN SAUCE

Duck is fat. It is not a failing but a fact. The good cook must find a way to remove much of that fat without drying out the meat. There are many techniques for this—steaming, then roasting; basting frequently with hot water or loosening the skin before cooking. However, a duck carefully prepared and carefully roasted in the classic manner consistently delivers crisp, mahogany skin and rich, succulent meat. Here the duck is served with a piquant brown sauce flavored with orange juice, orange peel, and green peppercorns.

1 duck, approximately 5 pounds
1 tablespoon vegetable oil
2 carrots, diced, divided
2 stalks celery, diced, divided
1 onion, diced, divided
½ cup dry white wine
3½ cups chicken stock
6 whole black peppercorns
1 bay leaf
1 clove garlic, smashed
1 clove
1½ teaspoons chopped, fresh thyme or
½ teaspoon dried thyme

Salt
Freshly ground, white pepper
1 tablespoon soy sauce
1 tablespoon honey
1 orange
1½ teaspoons cornstarch, dissolved in
1 tablespoon cold water
1 tablespoon green peppercorns, crushed
1 tablespoon butter
½ cup sliced, natural almonds, toasted

Remove wing tips from duck. Cut duck along each side of backbone to remove bone. Chop wing tips, backbone, neck, and giblets (reserve liver for other use) into small pieces. Brown in hot oil. Add one-half the vegetables and sauté until light brown. Deglaze with white wine. Add chicken stock, black peppercorns, bay leaf, garlic, clove, and thyme. Simmer, skimming occasionally, about 2 hours. Strain. Degrease stock. Reduce stock or add water, as necessary, to make 2 cups. Meanwhile, remove any loose fat from duck. Season duck with salt and pepper. Prick skin well around thighs, back and lower breast. Rub duck with mixture of soy sauce and honey. Place duck, breast-side up, on rack in a roasting pan with remaining vegetables. Bake at 425° F. for 15 minutes to brown lightly. Reduce heat to 350° F. and continue cooking 30 to 45 minutes longer. Juices should run pale pink for medium-rare or pale yellow for medium. Let duck rest 15 minutes, covered with a tea towel. To finish sauce, remove fat from roasting pan and place pan on top of stove. Deglaze with duck stock, scraping up brown bits. Strain into saucepan. Grate orange peel, then juice orange. Add 1 teaspoon orange peel, orange juice, cornstarch dissolved in water, green peppercorns, ¼ teaspoon salt,* and ¼ teaspoon white pepper. Simmer 5 minutes or until sauce thickens and lightly coats the back of a spoon. Remove from heat. Swirl in butter. Stir in almonds.

4 servings.

*If using canned chicken stock, omit salt.

In the current culinary celebration of American ingredients, bourbon is being given an honorable place as, if not the spirit of choice, at least a spirit worthy of exploration. Bourbon cookies, bourbon cakes, bourbon pies, and bourbon sauces abound. Here bourbon animates a simple sauce of reduced cream and tomato paste. With a bit of bite from lemon, freshly ground pepper, and cayenne, the sauce brings out the best in the delicately flavored filet. For less luxurious purses, it turns ground-beef patties into a special dish.

⅔ cup blanched, slivered almonds

3 tablespoons butter, divided

4 filet steaks, about 6 ounces each

½ cup bourbon

1 tablespoon tomato paste

½ cup heavy cream

½ teaspoon lemon juice

¼ teaspoon salt

⅛ teaspoon freshly ground, white pepper

Pinch cayenne

Sauté almonds in 1 tablespoon butter until golden; reserve. Sauté steaks in 1 tablespoon butter 2 to 3 minutes on each side for medium-rare; remove and reserve. Add bourbon to pan and ignite by touching the edge of the pan with the flame of a match. Allow to burn until flame dies out. Always use caution when flaming. Add tomato paste and stir until smooth. Add cream and reduce until sauce thickens and coats the back of a spoon. Add lemon juice, salt, white pepper, and cayenne. Whisk in remaining 1 tablespoon butter. Fold in almonds. Return meat to pan and just heat through.

4 servings.

FILET OF BEEF WITH ALMONDS, ROQUEFORT, AND OLIVES

This recipe produces a simple, unusual, and elegant entree. Thin slices of filet are garnished with a savory topping of almonds, olives, and Roquefort cheese. It is a beef eater's delight; the topping contrasts perfectly with the rich, fine-textured meat.

2-pound piece of filet of beef
4 teaspoons olive oil, divided
Salt
Freshly ground, black pepper
¼ cup chopped shallots

¼ cup dry (fino) sherry
1 ounce Roquefort cheese, crumbled
½ cup blanched, slivered almonds, toasted
¼ cup sliced, spiced green olives

Rub filet with 3 teaspoons olive oil; let rest at room temperature 1 hour. Season with salt and pepper. Preheat oven to 500° F. and place a 13 x 9 x 2-inch baking pan in oven to heat. Remove from oven and place filet in hot pan. Bake 5 minutes at 500° F. Reduce heat to 450° F. and continue baking 35 minutes or until internal temperature of meat reaches 125° F. (medium-rare). Remove from oven and allow to rest 10 minutes. Meanwhile, in a small skillet, sauté shallots until golden in remaining 1 teaspoon oil. Deglaze with sherry. Stir in Roquefort. Add almonds and olives; cook for 1 minute. To serve, thinly slice filet and spoon almond mixture down center of slices.

4 servings.

GRILLED STEAK WITH ALMOND VINAIGRETTE

This pungent and unctuous sauce of Spanish origin is an unusual accompaniment to steak. If you can grill the beef over charcoal, so much the better. Try it with grilled chicken, too.

2 cloves garlic, chopped finely

Salt

½ cup blanched, whole almonds, toasted

½ teaspoon red pepper flakes

2 tablespoons red wine vinegar

½ cup + 1 tablespoon olive oil

1½ pounds top sirloin or flank steak

Freshly ground, black pepper

Combine garlic, ½ teaspoon salt, almonds, red pepper flakes, and red wine vinegar in food processor or blender; purée. With machine running, slowly add ½ cup oil; chill several hours or overnight. Bring sauce to room temperature. Season steak with salt and pepper. Sear steak in remaining 1 tablespoon oil; reduce heat to medium and cook 2 to 3 minutes on each side for medium-rare. Slice thinly on the diagonal. Drizzle with almond vinaigrette.

4 to 6 servings.

VEAL CHOPS WITH CHARTREUSE BUTTER

Veal seems to be less popular in this country than beef, lamb, and pork. The expense of good veal is one reason, and a lack of understanding its preparation is another. Veal is quite lean and must be prepared in a way that prevents overcooking and thus drying out. In this recipe, thick chops are sealed with a coating of ground almonds and bread crumbs, then cooked quickly in a hot oven. The result is a succulent piece of meat that justifies its cost. In this recipe green Chartreuse adds an interesting, herbaceous note; however, Grand Marnier, brandy or even white wine are alternatives.

4 tablespoons butter, softened

1 teaspoon finely chopped shallots

4 tablespoons green Chartreuse liqueur, divided

Salt

½ cup blanched, whole almonds, toasted

¼ cup fresh, white bread crumbs

1 tablespoon chopped, fresh parsley

4 veal loin chops, ¾-inch thick

Freshly ground, black pepper

1 egg, beaten

Combine butter, shallots, 1 tablespoon Chartreuse, and ¼ teaspoon salt; form into a cylinder 1-inch in diameter and chill. Finely grind almonds in food processor or blender. Combine with bread crumbs, parsley, ½ teaspoon salt, and 1 tablespoon Chartreuse; reserve. Sprinkle chops on each side with remaining 2 tablespoons Chartreuse; let stand 10 minutes. Season each chop with salt and pepper. Dip each chop in egg, then in almond mixture. Place on rack in a roasting pan. Bake at 500° F. for 15 minutes. Slice seasoned butter into 8 slices. Place 2 slices butter on each chop. 4 servings.

VEAL SCALLOPS WITH ALMONDS AND CALVADOS

Sautéed veal scallops with heavy cream and the apple aroma of Calvados are reminiscent of the cooking of Normandy. Cognac or American brandy can be substituted, but the dish will lose a little finesse. Buy only the very best veal and treat it gently.

1 pound veal scallops
 Salt
 Freshly ground, white pepper
 Flour
3 tablespoons butter
1 tablespoon vegetable oil
2 shallots, chopped finely
1 clove garlic, chopped finely

½ cup Calvados or apple brandy
¼ cup dry white wine
1 cup heavy cream
2 teaspoons lemon juice
 Pinch freshly grated nutmeg
¾ cup sliced, natural almonds, toasted, divided

Season veal with salt and pepper. Dredge in flour; shake off excess. Sauté veal in mixture of butter and oil over medium-high heat, 1 minute on each side. Remove and keep warm. In fat remaining in pan, sauté shallots and garlic. Deglaze with Calvados, and ignite by touching the edge of the pan with the flame of a match. Allow to burn until flame dies out. Always use caution when flaming. Add white wine. Reduce over medium-high heat to a syrupy consistency. Add cream and reduce until mixture thickens slightly and coats the back of a spoon, about 3 to 4 minutes. Season with ½ teaspoon salt and ⅛ teaspoon pepper. Stir in lemon juice and nutmeg, then ½ cup almonds. Return veal to pan and heat 1 minute. If sauce is too thick, add 2 to 3 teaspoons boiling water. Garnish with remaining ¼ cup almonds.

6 servings.

VEAL STEW WITH GREEN ONION AND ALMONDS

Here's a briefly simmered veal stew finished with orange peel, Chartreuse, and the bite of green onions. It answers to those who feel white stews or blanquettes are insipid.

⅔ cup blanched, slivered almonds

3 tablespoons butter, divided

1½ pounds boneless veal from leg, cut into strips 1½ x ½ x ¼-inch

Salt

Freshly ground, white pepper

2 tablespoons vegetable oil

¾ cup dry white wine

½ cup heavy cream

3 bunches green onions, white portion only, sliced ½-inch thick

2 tablespoons green Chartreuse liqueur

⅛ teaspoon grated orange peel

Sauté almonds in 1 tablespoon butter until golden; reserve. Season veal with salt and pepper. Sauté in remaining 2 tablespoons butter and oil until browned. Add wine and bring to a simmer. Stir in cream; cover and cook 20 minutes, stirring frequently. If necessary, uncover and reduce until sauce thickens and coats the back of a spoon, 2 to 3 minutes. Add green onions, Chartreuse, and orange peel; cook 5 minutes. Stir in almonds.

6 servings.

LAMB CHOPS WITH ALMOND-PARMESAN CHEESE COATING

Lamb is quite expensive these days, and the quality varies a great deal. Consequently, it is worth seeking out a good butcher to insure you get what you pay for. The chops in this recipe are baked quickly in a crusty coating perfumed with lemon peel and garlic. They emerge from the oven juicy and flavorful. For convenience, they may be coated and held in the refrigerator for up to an hour.

½ cup blanched, whole almonds, toasted

½ cup fresh, white bread crumbs

⅓ cup freshly grated, Parmesan cheese

2 tablespoons chopped, fresh parsley

½ teaspoon grated lemon peel

2 cloves garlic, chopped finely

8 single-rib lamb chops

Salt

Freshly ground, black pepper

1 egg, beaten with 1 teaspoon water

Finely grind almonds in food processor or blender. Combine with next five ingredients; reserve. Season lamb chops with salt and pepper. Dip each chop into egg and coat well with almond mixture. Preheat a roasting pan and rack in a 500° F. oven. Place chops on hot rack. Bake at 500° F. for 12 to 15 minutes for medium-rare. Test lamb chops by making a small slit near the bone to see if meat is done.

4 servings.

RACK OF LAMB WITH ALMOND MADEIRA SAUCE

Crisp, sautéed almonds add a new dimension to this rack of lamb with classic Madeira sauce.

1 rack of lamb (8 chops) with trimmings

Salt

Freshly ground, black pepper

Lamb Stock

Trimmings from rack

1 tablespoon vegetable oil

1 tablespoon butter

2 stalks celery, diced

1 carrot, peeled, and diced

1 onion, chopped

¾ teaspoon chopped, fresh thyme or ¼ teaspoon dried thyme

1 clove garlic, chopped finely

4 black peppercorns

1 bay leaf

¼ teaspoon chopped, fresh rosemary or pinch dried rosemary

2 teaspoons tomato paste

⅔ cup dry white wine

4 cups water

Madeira Sauce

½ cup chopped, natural almonds

4 tablespoons butter, divided

¼ cup Madeira wine

2 teaspoons cornstarch, dissolved in 2 tablespoons water

¼ teaspoon chopped, fresh rosemary or pinch dried rosemary

¼ teaspoon salt

¼ teaspoon freshly ground, black pepper

Reserve rack and brown lamb trimmings in mixture of oil and butter. Add celery, carrot, and onion; sauté until lightly browned. Add next six ingredients; cook 1 minute. Add white wine and water; simmer 1 hour. Degrease stock. Strain and reduce liquid to 1 cup; reserve. Season rack of lamb with salt and pepper. Bake at 425° F. for 15 to 20 minutes or until instant-reading thermometer reads 125° F. for medium-rare. While lamb is cooking, prepare Madeira sauce. Sauté almonds in 2 tablespoons butter until crisp. Add Madeira and reduce by one quarter. Add lamb stock. Stir in cornstarch dissolved in water. Stir in remaining 2 tablespoons butter, rosemary, salt, and pepper; remove from heat. Remove lamb from oven and cover with clean tea towel and let rest for 15 minutes. Carve into chops. Drizzle sauce over lamb.

4 servings.

LAMB APRICOT CURRY

In this moderately spicy lamb curry, the fruit sauce is simmered separately. At the last moment, the lamb is browned quickly and added to the sauce for a brief warming. The result is rich, juicy, flavorful meat supported perfectly by the tart, spicy sauce. Sautéed almonds are a texture and flavor bridge between the two.

1 cup blanched, slivered almonds

4 tablespoons butter, divided

2 cups finely chopped onion

1 teaspoon sugar

3 tablespoons vegetable oil, divided

4 cloves garlic, chopped finely

½ cup dried apricots, chopped finely

¼ cup raisins

1 tablespoon curry powder

1 teaspoon ground cumin

Pinch cayenne

2 cups beef stock

1 cup water

1½ pounds boneless lamb from leg, cut into strips, 1½ x ½ x ¼-inch

1 teaspoon salt

1 teaspoon freshly ground, black pepper

Sauté almonds in 1 tablespoon butter until golden; reserve. Sauté onion with sugar in 1 tablespoon butter and 1 tablespoon oil until lightly colored. Add garlic, apricots, raisins, curry powder, cumin, and cayenne; cook 2 minutes longer. Deglaze with beef stock. Add water and simmer sauce until thickened, about 10 to 12 minutes. When sauce is almost done, sear lamb in batches in remaining 2 tablespoons butter and 2 tablespoons oil. Add almonds and lamb to sauce; heat through. Season with salt and pepper.

4 servings.

PORK CHOPS WITH ORANGE GLAZE

A fear of undercooking pork causes much of it to emerge from the kitchen dry and tasteless. Currently, pigs are fed better diets than those of previous generations and are safer to eat. Happily for diet-conscious diners, today's pork also has a higher percentage of lean meat. Make sure these chops are thoroughly cooked, but please don't ruin their delicate taste and tender texture by overcooking. This recipe delivers juicy chops redolent of garlic, ginger, and sesame oil in a glaze of orange juice and red onion.

3 cloves garlic, chopped finely

1 teaspoon grated, fresh ginger or ¼ teaspoon powdered ginger

1 teaspoon freshly ground, black pepper

2 tablespoons Oriental sesame oil, divided

1 tablespoon peanut oil

4 pork loin chops, about 1-inch thick

½ cup blanched, slivered almonds

1⅓ cups diced red onion

1½ cups fresh orange juice

½ teaspoon salt

4 tablespoons butter

Combine garlic, ginger, pepper, and 1 tablespoon sesame oil. Rub into pork chops and let marinate 30 minutes at room temperature. In remaining 1 tablespoon sesame oil and peanut oil, brown pork chops, 2 to 3 minutes on each side. Reduce heat and continue to cook, 3 to 4 minutes on each side or until chops are tender; remove and reserve. Add almonds to pan and sauté until golden. Add onions and sauté until translucent. Stir in orange juice and reduce over high heat 4 to 5 minutes or until of a syrupy consistency. Reduce heat and stir in salt and butter. Add pork chops and heat through.

4 servings.

PORK RAGOUT WITH CURRY AND COCONUT

Here is a succulent pork stew with a Caribbean influence. The meat cooks in the spicy sauce and becomes infused with the flavors of curry, rum, and coconut. A marvelous buffet dish, it reheats well and even benefits from a day or two of mellowing.

⅔ cup blanched, slivered almonds

3 tablespoons butter, divided

2 pounds pork butt or shoulder, cubed

2 tablespoons flour

1 onion, chopped coarsely

1 clove garlic, chopped finely

½ cup dry white wine

½ cup dark rum

1 cup beef stock

½ cup shredded coconut

2 tablespoons honey

1 teaspoon curry powder

½ teaspoon salt

⅛ teaspoon cayenne

Sauté almonds in 1 tablespoon butter until golden; reserve. Dredge pork in flour; shake off excess. Sauté pork in 1 tablespoon butter until browned; reserve. Sauté onion in remaining 1 tablespoon butter until translucent; add garlic. Deglaze pan with white wine. Add rum and ignite by touching the edge of the pan with the flame of a match. Allow to burn until flame dies out. Always use caution when flaming. Add beef stock, coconut, honey, curry powder, salt, and cayenne. Add pork and cook over medium heat, 30 to 40 minutes, until sauce is thickened and meat is tender. Stir in almonds.

6 to 8 servings.

HONEY CUMIN PORK WITH RICE

The combination of honey and cumin, reminiscent of the Middle East, infuses pork and rice with a wonderful warmth in this baked mélange. Serve an astringent salad of bitter greens dressed in lemon vinaigrette to complement the richness of the meat and the heady flavors.

⅔ cup blanched, slivered almonds

3 tablespoons olive oil, divided

2 tablespoons butter

1½ pounds boneless pork loin, cut into 1-inch cubes

1 onion, chopped

2 cloves garlic, chopped finely

½ cup coarsely grated carrots

½ cup dry white wine

3 tablespoons honey

2½ teaspoons ground cumin

½ teaspoon salt

1 cup long grain rice

1½ cups chicken stock

Sauté almonds in 1 tablespoon oil until golden; reserve. Add remaining 2 tablespoons oil and butter to pan. Brown pork cubes; remove and reserve. In oil remaining in pan, sauté onion until translucent. Add garlic and carrot; sauté 1 minute. Deglaze with wine. Stir in honey, cumin, and salt. Add rice and cook, stirring, 2 minutes. Add chicken stock and bring to a boil. Bake, uncovered, at 400° F. on lowest rack in oven for 20 minutes. Place pork cubes on top. Continue baking 10 minutes longer or until all liquid is absorbed and pork is cooked through. Remove from oven and let rest 5 minutes. Stir in almonds.

4 servings.

ITALIAN SAUSAGE AND RICE

This dish is an American first cousin to Italian risotto. It uses our own long grain rice and a simplified cooking method but still produces a creamy rice dish that is punctuated by the bite of hot Italian sausage and the astringency of fresh sage. Perfect for before or after the theater, brunch, lunch or Sunday-night supper, its richness requires only the company of a green salad with fresh fruit and the merest wisp of a butter cookie for dessert.

½ pound hot Italian sausage

1 onion, chopped

2 tablespoons butter

1 cup long grain rice

½ cup dry white wine

1 cup chicken stock

1 tablespoon finely chopped, fresh sage or 1 teaspoon dried sage

½ cup freshly grated Parmesan cheese

½ cup blanched, slivered almonds, toasted

¼ cup heavy cream

2 tablespoons chopped, fresh parsley

Remove sausage from casing and crumble. Sauté sausage and onion in butter over medium-high heat until sausage is brown and onion translucent. Add rice and sauté 1 minute. Add white wine, chicken stock, and sage. Bring to a boil, cover, and reduce to a simmer. Cook 20 minutes or until all liquid is absorbed. Remove from heat and let stand 5 minutes. Stir in Parmesan cheese, almonds, cream, and parsley. Cover and let stand 2 to 3 minutes longer.

4 servings.

SHERRIED SAUSAGE

Bites of sausage, green onion, and toasted almonds, glazed with a mixture of cream sherry and orange juice, make a rich, and, quite frankly, yummy brunch dish. Serve it with creamy scrambled eggs or crisp waffles or hash browned sweet potatoes with lots of freshly ground white pepper.

¾ cup cream (sweet) sherry, divided

1 pound pork sausage links, cut into thirds

½ cup blanched, slivered almonds, toasted

½ cup sliced green onions

¼ cup fresh orange juice

Pour ½ cup sherry over sausage, cover, and simmer 10 minutes. Drain off excess fat. Continue to cook sausage, uncovered, turning frequently, until brown and glazed. Add almonds and green onions; sauté, stirring frequently, for 1 minute. Add remaining ¼ cup sherry and orange juice to pan and reduce by half or until of a syrupy consistency.

4 servings.

SHRIMP WITH CUMIN AND LIME

Cumin and lime add South-of-the-Border notes to another shrimp sauté. Serve this with buttered mellone (tiny, rice-shaped pasta) as a main course or for starters, with garlic toast made from thin slices of French bread.

3 tablespoons chopped shallots

2 tablespoons butter, divided

1 tablespoon vegetable oil

1 teaspoon ground cumin

1½ pounds medium, raw shrimp, peeled and deveined

¼ cup lime juice

2 tablespoons dry white wine

½ teaspoon salt

¼ teaspoon freshly ground, white pepper

½ cup blanched, slivered almonds, toasted

Sauté shallots in 1 tablespoon butter and oil until translucent. Add cumin. Add shrimp and sauté until just firm, about 2 to 3 minutes. Add lime juice and wine. Reduce liquid over high heat to a syrupy glaze. Stir in salt, pepper, and almonds. Remove from heat and stir in remaining 1 tablespoon butter.

4 to 6 servings.

SHRIMP AND PEPPERS

Good quality shrimp is available throughout the land these days, but unless one lives in shrimp-boat country, it is unlikely to be fresh. Instead, it has been frozen and subsequently defrosted. If flash frozen immediately after catching, shrimp loses little in flavor or texture. Beware of defrosted shrimp that have been sitting for too long in the glass case at the store. The only insurance is to know your fishmonger and to use your nose. Good shrimp has a faint odor of the sea. If you smell ammonia and fishy odors, leave immediately. In this recipe, the visual delight of red and green, the crunch of sautéed almonds, and the piquancy of fresh herbs and lemon come together in a perfectly balanced sauté fit for company.

It requires not much more than one-half hour to prepare from start to finish and is equally at home as the first course or the main event. Serve it with California Sauvignon Blanc and warm, sourdough bread.

3 tablespoons lemon juice, divided

3 cloves garlic, chopped finely

⅛ teaspoon red pepper flakes

½ teaspoon freshly ground, black pepper

1 tablespoon olive oil

1½ pounds medium, raw shrimp, peeled and deveined

¾ cup blanched, slivered almonds

4 tablespoons butter, divided

1 red bell pepper, julienned

2 tablespoons thinly sliced chives

2 tablespoons chopped, fresh parsley

2 tablespoons chopped, fresh basil or 2 teaspoons dried basil

½ teaspoon salt

1 lemon for garnish

Combine 2 tablespoons lemon juice and next four ingredients; marinate shrimp in mixture for 15 minutes at room temperature. Sauté almonds in 2 tablespoons butter until they begin to turn golden. Add shrimp and red bell pepper; sauté 2 to 3 minutes until shrimp are just tender. Remove from heat and stir in herbs, salt, remaining 1 tablespoon lemon juice, and remaining 2 tablespoons butter. Garnish with lemon wedges.

4 to 6 servings.

SAFFRON SCALLOPS WITH VEGETABLE MEDLEY

In this recipe scallops enter the classic marriage of seafood and saffron. Matchstick pieces of carrot, celery, and turnip give the dish a contemporary flavor and add color and crunch.

¾ cup blanched, slivered almonds

3 tablespoons butter, divided

2 carrots, peeled and julienned

1 large stalk celery, julienned

1 small turnip, peeled and julienned

1 teaspoon olive oil

2 tablespoons finely chopped shallots

1 clove garlic, chopped finely

2 tablespoons dry white wine

1 pound scallops (if large, slice into medallions)

2 tablespoons heavy cream

2 tablespoons sour cream

1 tablespoon chopped, fresh tarragon or 1 teaspoon dried tarragon

1 teaspoon salt

2 large pinches saffron threads or ¼ teaspoon powdered saffron, dissolved in 1 teaspoon hot water

Sauté almonds in 1 tablespoon butter until golden; reserve. Plunge carrots, celery, and turnips into salted, boiling water. When water returns to a boil, remove vegetables and drain; reserve. In remaining 2 tablespoons butter and the oil, sauté shallots and garlic until translucent. Deglaze with white wine. Add scallops and simmer gently 1 minute. Add cream and reduce 1 minute. Stir in sour cream, tarragon, salt, saffron, vegetables, and almonds. Heat through.

4 servings.

SCALLOPS WITH MUSHROOMS AND SCOTCH WHISKY

Scallops are a bit pricey but little is wasted and, prepared properly, are worth every penny. Remove the small piece of muscle attached to the scallop, if it is there, for it is often filled with sand. Although similar in appearance to the scallop itself, it is obviously separate. Don't confuse it with the crescent-shaped coral, should you be fortunate enough to find scallops with these. If you do, treasure the coral and treat it like the scallop. Be sure to rinse all briefly under cold water and pat dry thoroughly. In this sauté of scallops with mushrooms, the glaze of butter, Scotch whisky, and a touch of Dijon mustard provides a contrast to the sweet meat of the shellfish.

2 tablespoons finely chopped shallots

3 tablespoons butter, divided

1 tablespoon vegetable oil

1 pound scallops (if large, slice into medallions)

¼ pound mushrooms, quartered

¼ cup Scotch whisky

2 teaspoons Dijon mustard

½ cup blanched, slivered almonds, toasted

½ teaspoon salt

¼ teaspoon freshly ground, white pepper

Sauté shallots in 2 tablespoons butter and oil until golden, about 1 minute. Add scallops and sauté over high heat until almost done, about 2 to 3 minutes. Add mushrooms to scallops, continue to cook over high heat, stirring constantly, 1 minute. Deglaze pan with whisky and ignite by touching the edge of the pan with the flame of a match. Allow to burn until flame dies out. Always use caution when flaming. Stir in mustard and add almonds. Remove from heat and stir in remaining 1 tablespoon butter. Season with salt and pepper.

4 servings.

ALMOND FENNEL FILET OF SOLE

Fish and fennel have a delicious affinity for each other. Here a touch of licorice flavor permeates a rich sauce of cream, wine, tomato bits, and toasted almonds. The fish is delicious and visually appealing simply poached and sauced, but a quick pass under a hot broiler adds a fine glaze.

4 filets of sole, 6 to 8 ounces each

Sauce

1½ cups heavy cream

¼ cup chopped shallots

1 teaspoon fennel seeds, crushed

2 tablespoons butter

2 teaspoons flour

½ cup dry white wine

1 large tomato, peeled, seeded, diced, and well-drained

½ teaspoon salt

¼ teaspoon freshly ground, white pepper

1 cup sliced, natural almonds, toasted

Poaching Liquid

¼ cup butter

¼ cup dry white wine

1 shallot, sliced

¼ teaspoon fennel seeds, crushed

Reserve fish filets and prepare sauce. In heavy saucepan, reduce cream to 1 cup; reserve. Sauté shallots and fennel seeds in butter until shallots are translucent. Sprinkle flour over shallots and fennel seeds; cook, stirring, 1 minute. Gradually stir in wine and cook until slightly thickened. Add reduced cream, a little at a time, stirring constantly. Add tomato, a little at a time, stirring constantly. Simmer to reduce sauce until 1½ cups remain. Season with salt and pepper. Reserve. Combine poaching liquid ingredients and simmer 5 to 10 minutes to meld flavors. Poach filets in simmering liquid until just firm. Drain filets well. Reheat sauce, if necessary; add ¾ cup almonds. Pour ¼ cup sauce over each filet and garnish each serving with 1 tablespoon remaining almonds.

4 servings.

SOLE WITH VERMOUTH CREAM SAUCE

This recipe is an adaptation of a delicious dish created by the Troisgros brothers. Ground almonds, as the principal breading ingredient, add the special texture and flavor that distinguishes this version. This recipe is simple to execute, although one must get used to the idea of the coated filets.

½ cup dry white wine

1 shallot, chopped finely

¾ cup blanched, whole almonds, lightly toasted and ground

¼ cup bread crumbs

4 sole filets, 6 to 8 ounces each

8 tablespoons butter, melted

3 tablespoons dry vermouth

1 cup heavy cream

½ teaspoon Dijon mustard

½ teaspoon salt

¼ teaspoon freshly ground, white pepper

1 tablespoon lemon juice

2 teaspoons chopped, fresh tarragon or 1 teaspoon dried tarragon

Combine white wine and shallots in a shallow baking dish large enough to lay fish filets flat without overlapping; reserve. Combine ground almonds and bread crumbs; reserve. Dip fish filets in butter, then press topside in almond-crumb mixture. Place filets in the baking dish, crumb side up, being careful not to let crumbs get moistened by wine mixture. Drizzle remaining melted butter over filets; bake at 425° F. for 15 minutes. Carefully remove fish and keep warm. Pour pan liquids into saucepan and add vermouth. Reduce over medium heat until 2 tablespoons liquid remain. Add cream and reduce until sauce thickens and coats the back of a spoon. Stir in mustard, salt, and pepper. Stir in lemon juice. Divide sauce evenly among four heated plates. Sprinkle with tarragon. Place fish filets on top.

4 servings.

ALMOND SOLE WITH LIME-GINGER BUTTER

Sole can be a boring fish. With its fine texture and mild—some would say lack of—flavor, it seems sometimes little more than a transporter of sauces. Here a crusting of almonds and a piquant dab of compound butter play point and counterpoint to the delicacy of the fish. Little potatoes sautéed or steamed, or a simple rice pilaf, complete the fresh simplicity of this dish.

¾ cup butter, softened, divided

½ lime, juiced

1 teaspoon grated, fresh ginger or ¼ teaspoon powdered ginger

Salt

1 cup sliced, natural almonds, lightly toasted

4 filets of sole, 6 to 8 ounces each

Freshly ground, white pepper

4 thin lime slices

Combine ½ cup butter, lime juice, ginger, and ¼ teaspoon salt. Shape into a log 1-inch in diameter. Chill. Lightly crush almonds with hands to break into small pieces. Reserve. Season filets with salt and pepper. Dip filets in remaining ¼ cup butter, melted. Press topside of filets in almonds; place topside up on buttered sheet pan. Bake at 500° F. for 5 to 10 minutes or until just firm. Top each serving with 2 slices of lime-ginger butter and 1 lime slice.

4 servings.

TROUT WITH ALMOND AND MUSTARD SAUCE

With the advent of trout farms and modern transportation, fresh trout is readily available throughout the land. Yet, it is still underutilized by a population in love with the anonymous filet. For the squeamish, the heads can be removed by the fishmonger or the cook prior to preparation. When sautéed, the meat is sweet and succulent, if a bit different from wild trout. In this recipe, crisp, browned whole trout take on a Scandinavian guise dressed in a sauce redolent of mustard, honey, and dill.

4 trout, cleaned
Flour
4 tablespoons vegetable oil, divided
½ cup finely chopped shallots
2 cups dry white wine
6 tablespoons Dijon mustard
4 tablespoons butter

2 teaspoons chopped, fresh dill or ½ teaspoon dried dill
1 teaspoon honey
¼ teaspoon freshly ground, white pepper
¼ teaspoon salt
⅔ cup sliced, natural almonds, toasted

Lightly dredge trout in flour and pat off excess. Brown trout over high heat in 2 tablespoons oil. Reduce heat to medium and cook trout 2 to 3 minutes on each side or until just tender; remove trout and keep warm. Add remaining 2 tablespoons oil to pan and sauté shallots until translucent. Add wine and reduce liquid by half. Stir in mustard, butter, dill, honey, pepper, salt, and almonds. Drizzle sauce over trout. 4 servings.

BAKED HALIBUT FILETS WITH TOMATOED BEARNAISE SAUCE

The contrast of the sweet, firm flesh of the halibut with the piquant, rich texture of the tomatoed béarnaise excites the senses. After a brief stint in the oven, the fish emerges moist and delicate, topped by a glazed, almond-studded sauce. Of course, this presupposes impeccable fish.

½ cup chopped, natural almonds

1 tablespoon butter

1 small tomato, peeled, seeded, and drained

1 tablespoon chopped, fresh tarragon or 1 teaspoon dried tarragon

⅓ cup dry white wine

2 tablespoons white wine vinegar

1 shallot, chopped finely

1 egg yolk

1 teaspoon cold water

½ teaspoon salt

⅓ cup butter, melted

4 pieces halibut filet, 6 to 8 ounces each

Sauté almonds in butter until crisp; reserve. In food processor or blender, purée tomato; add tarragon and reserve. Combine wine, vinegar, and shallots in saucepan. Reduce over medium heat until about 2 tablespoons of liquid remain. Strain into top of double boiler and cool. Over simmering water, beat in egg yolk, water, and salt until slightly thickened. Add butter by drops, whisking constantly. Stir in tomato purée and almonds. Top halibut filets with sauce. Bake at 550° F. for 8 to 10 minutes or until firm.

4 servings.

ROCK COD WITH JALAPENO SALSA

Contrary to the filet-of-sole school of thought, all fish is not delicate, destined to be blanketed by a butter or cream sauce. Here is robust rock cod topped by a snappy salsa, in the Mexican mode. The sauce can be made ahead, and the filets also take kindly to a charcoal fire, if available.

½ cup + 2 tablespoons olive oil, divided

4 cloves garlic, chopped finely

1 teaspoon salt, divided

2 tablespoons chopped, fresh thyme or ¾ teaspoon dried thyme

4 rock cod filets, about 6 to 8 ounces each

1 onion, chopped

¼ cup sliced green olives

3 pickled jalapeño peppers, seeded and chopped

½ cup julienned red bell pepper

¼ cup lime juice

¼ cup orange juice

½ teaspoon orange peel

⅔ cup sliced, natural almonds, toasted

Combine ¼ cup oil, garlic, ½ teaspoon salt, and thyme. Coat filets on both sides with oil mixture; marinate 30 minutes. Bake fish at 450° F. for 8 to 10 minutes or until fish is just firm. While fish is baking, sauté onions in ¼ cup oil until translucent. Add olives, jalapeño peppers, red bell pepper, lime juice, orange juice and peel. Reduce over medium heat 3 to 5 minutes to a syrupy consistency; add remaining 2 tablespoons oil. Stir in almonds. Spoon sauce over filets.

4 servings.

FILET OF COD WITH GARLIC MAYONNAISE AND GREEN CHILES

Here's a contemporary version of the classic pairing—filet of fish and almonds. Garlic mayonnaise, in the French tradition, spiked with green chiles in the California style, makes a pungent topping for baked fish. The toasted, sliced almonds marry deliciously with these savory elements and add an important textural dimension to the dish. Rice pilaf with bits of tomato and sautéed yellow squash are tasty in the supporting roles.

2 large cloves garlic

Salt

Freshly ground, white pepper

¼ cup finely chopped, peeled fresh chiles or ¼ cup finely chopped canned green chiles, divided

1½ teaspoons lime juice

1 egg yolk

⅓ cup olive oil

⅓ cup vegetable oil

1½ pounds cod filets or any firm white filet

¾ cup sliced, natural almonds

With a mortar and pestle, or with a fork in a bowl, mash together the garlic, ¾ teaspoon salt, ⅛ teaspoon pepper, and 2 tablespoons green chiles. Add lime juice, then beat in egg yolk. Slowly beat in oils. Lightly salt and pepper fish filets and arrange in single layer in greased ovenproof baking dish. Fold almonds and remaining 2 tablespoons chiles gently into sauce and spoon sauce over fish. Bake at 450° F. for 5 to 7 minutes or until fish is firm.

4 servings.

TUNA STEAKS WITH TOMATOES, ONIONS, AND GARLIC

Perhaps tuna is best known as it comes from the can, destined for generations of tuna salad sandwiches. On the other hand, fresh tuna is another matter entirely and one worth investigating. In this easily prepared dish, the sturdy flavor of fresh tuna steaks basks in the savory surroundings of garlic, onions, tomatoes, and, although a bit unusual, prunes and almonds.

½ cup blanched, slivered almonds
5 tablespoons olive oil, divided
2 onions, sliced thinly
2 cloves garlic, chopped finely
2 tomatoes, peeled, seeded, diced, and drained
½ cup dry white wine
1 teaspoon salt
3 anchovy filets, chopped
1 cup prunes, sliced
¼ teaspoon red pepper flakes
1½ pounds tuna filets

Sauté almonds in 1 tablespoon oil; reserve. Sauté onions in 3 tablespoons oil until translucent. Add garlic. Add tomatoes, white wine, and salt. Simmer until liquid is reduced, about 3 to 5 minutes. Fold in anchovies, prunes, red pepper flakes, and almonds. Brush fish with remaining 1 tablespoon oil. Arrange fish in one layer in baking dish. Spoon sauce over. Bake at 350° F. for 15 to 20 minutes or until fish is just firm.

4 servings.

SALMON FILETS WITH RED BELL PEPPER VINAIGRETTE

The flavorful taste of fresh salmon, its meaty texture, and its distinctive color make it a gastronomical delight. In this recipe, salmon filets are topped with a thick, red bell pepper vinaigrette. The sweet, slightly charred flavor of the roasted pepper combines with balsamic vinegar and fruity olive oil to create a delicious complement to the fish.

2 large, red bell peppers

⅔ cup blanched, slivered almonds

8 tablespoons olive oil, divided

4 pieces salmon filet, about 7 ounces each

Coarsely ground, black pepper

1 clove garlic

3 tablespoons balsamic vinegar

½ teaspoon salt

2 pinches cayenne

Roast peppers under broiler or on a long fork held over a gas flame, turning occasionally, until skin is blackened. Place in closed paper bag to steam for 10 minutes. Under cold running water, scrape blackened skin from peppers. Remove stem and seeds. Reserve peppers. Sauté almonds in 1 tablespoon oil until golden; reserve. Arrange salmon filets in a shallow baking dish. Generously season filets with coarsely ground, black pepper; reserve. Purée red bell peppers and garlic. Add vinegar, salt, and cayenne. Slowly beat in remaining 7 tablespoons oil. Fold in almonds. Pour mixture over fish. Bake at 500° F. for about 10 minutes or until fish is just firm.
4 servings.

ALMOND POUND CAKE

This dense, moist pound cake boasts the essence of almond flavor. It keeps well and invites topping with the likes of fresh fruit and sweet, heavy cream or almond ice cream and thick fudge sauce.

8 ounces blanched almond paste
1½ cups sugar
1½ cups butter, softened
9 eggs

1½ teaspoons vanilla
3 cups sifted flour
½ cup sliced, natural almonds

Knead almond paste with fingers until soft and pliable. Combine almond paste and sugar; add butter and beat until light and fluffy. Add eggs, one at a time, to almond-paste mixture. Add vanilla. Gradually beat in flour until smooth. Divide batter between two buttered and floured 9 x 5 x 3-inch loaf pans. Top each loaf with ¼ cup almonds. Bake at 325° F. for 1 hour or until toothpick inserted in center comes out clean. 2 loaves.

ALMOND LEMON POUND CAKE

The nutty flavor of toasted almonds and the tartness of fresh lemon juice contrast deliciously in this traditional pound cake. A final dousing with a vanilla-spiked lemon syrup intensifies flavors and adds a rich, moist quality.

2 cups cake flour

½ teaspoon cream of tartar

½ teaspoon salt

1 cup butter

1 cup sugar

4 eggs

5 tablespoons lemon juice, divided

1¼ cups chopped, natural almonds, toasted, divided

½ cup powdered sugar

½ teaspoon vanilla

Sift cake flour with cream of tartar and salt; reserve. Cream butter and sugar. Add eggs, one at a time, mixing well. Add 2 tablespoons lemon juice. Gradually add sifted ingredients; mix thoroughly. Fold in 1 cup almonds. Pour batter into a greased 9 x 5 x 3-inch loaf pan. Sprinkle top with remaining ¼ cup almonds. Bake at 325° F. for 1 hour or until toothpick inserted in center comes out clean. While cake is baking, combine powdered sugar, remaining 3 tablespoons lemon juice, and vanilla; heat, stirring to dissolve sugar. When cake is done, drizzle top with hot glaze. Let cake cool, then remove from pan.

1 loaf.

CHOCOLATE ALMOND CAKE

Here is a sinfully dense chocolate cake infused with the moist richness of almond paste. It excites the senses in a special way that only intensely chocolate deliciousness can. Having said that, one can only remark on the speed with which it disappears.

Cake

1 cup flour

1½ teaspoons baking soda

1 teaspoon salt

¾ cup blanched almond paste

1 cup sugar

½ cup butter, softened

4 eggs

1 teaspoon vanilla

8 ounces semisweet chocolate, melted and cooled

¾ cup sour cream

Fudge Frosting

½ cup butter

7 ounces semisweet chocolate

2 eggs, beaten

1 teaspoon vanilla

4 cups sifted powdered sugar

Line the bottoms of two 9-inch round cake pans with waxed paper; butter and flour. Sift together flour, baking soda, and salt; reserve. Knead almond paste with fingers until soft and pliable. Combine almond paste and sugar until mixture resembles coarse cornmeal. Add butter and beat, scraping down sides of bowl, until smooth. Beat in eggs, one at a time, then vanilla. Combine chocolate and sour cream and add alternately with flour mixture to almond-paste mixture, mixing well. Pour batter into prepared cake pans. Bake at 350° F. for 25 to 30 minutes or until cake springs back when touched lightly with finger. Cool in pans on wire rack 30 minutes. Remove from pans and cool completely. Prepare Fudge Frosting by melting butter and chocolate in top of double boiler over simmering water; cool. Beat in eggs and vanilla. Gradually beat in powdered sugar until smooth. Spread frosting between layers, on sides, and top. 10 to 12 servings.

ORANGE ALMOND CAKE

Buttercream icings are not the easiest to make, but if one remembers that the process is one of emulsion — much like hollandaise, it becomes easier. Like hollandaise, temperature is important, and the icing should not be too warm or too cold when the butter is beaten in. In this recipe a delicately textured orange and almond cake is topped with buttery, orange-liqueur-scented icing.

Cake

⅓ cup butter

½ cup + 2 tablespoons sugar, divided

2 eggs, separated

1 tablespoon orange liqueur

⅔ cup flour

1 teaspoon baking powder

1 teaspoon baking soda

¼ teaspoon salt

6 tablespoons sour cream

1 teaspoon grated orange peel

½ cup whole, natural almonds, toasted and finely chopped, divided

Buttercream Frosting

½ cup sugar

2½ tablespoons water

4 egg yolks, at room temperature, beaten

2 teaspoons orange liqueur

½ cup + 2 tablespoons butter, softened

To prepare cake, beat butter and ½ cup sugar until fluffy. Beat in egg yolks, one at a time, then 1 tablespoon orange liqueur; reserve. Mix flour, baking powder, baking soda, and salt. Add dry ingredients to butter mixture alternately with sour cream, beginning and ending with dry ingredients, beating until batter is smooth. Stir in orange peel and ¼ cup almonds; reserve. Beat egg whites with remaining 2 tablespoons sugar until stiff; fold into batter. Pour batter into a greased, 8-inch, round cake pan. Bake at 350° F. for 20 minutes or until toothpick inserted in center comes out clean. Cool 15 minutes; remove from pan and cool completely. Meanwhile, prepare Buttercream Frosting. Boil sugar and water until mixture reaches 234° F. (soft-ball stage). Immediately, while sugar mixture is very hot and liquid, rapidly add to beaten eggs in a thin, steady stream, whisking constantly, being careful not to get syrup on sides of bowl. Whisk in orange liqueur. Cool. Beat the butter on high speed about 3 minutes, until pale yellow and resembling the consistency of whipped cream. Beat in the cooled egg-yolk mixture, a little at a time, until smooth. Chill about 10 minutes. Ice top and sides of cake. Press remaining almonds around sides. If desired, decorate with buttercream rosettes and toasted whole, natural almonds.

8 to 10 servings.

DOUBLE ALMOND BRANDY CAKE

Almond paste and sour cream make this brandy-kissed cake a moist, dense delight. The crunch of sliced almonds adds texture and intensifies the almond flavor. It travels and keeps well, which makes it a welcomed visitor.

2 cups flour
1 teaspoon baking soda
1 teaspoon baking powder
¼ teaspoon salt
1 cup sugar
½ cup + 1 tablespoon butter, divided
2 eggs, beaten
1 teaspoon vanilla
1 cup sour cream
1½ cups sliced, natural almonds, toasted, divided

½ cup half-and-half
¼ cup brandy
1 can (8 ounces) blanched almond paste
4 tablespoons milk
4 tablespoons powdered sugar
Sliced, natural almonds, toasted, for garnish

Sift first four ingredients; reserve. Cream sugar and ½ cup butter. Add beaten eggs and vanilla; blend well. Add dry ingredients to butter mixture alternately with sour cream; batter will be stiff. Stir in 1 cup almonds; reserve. Combine half-and-half, brandy, and remaining ½ cup almonds; reserve. Knead almond paste with fingers until soft and pliable; add to brandy mixture a little at a time until well blended (mixture will be slightly lumpy). Spread one-half of the cake batter in a greased and floured 9 or 10-inch tube pan. Spread one-half of almond-paste mixture over cake batter. Spread remaining batter over paste layer. To remaining almond-paste mixture, add milk and powdered sugar. Pour over cake. Bake at 350° F. for 30 minutes. Remove from oven and garnish top with sliced almonds. Bake 30 minutes longer or until toothpick inserted in center comes out clean. Cool on wire rack 30 minutes. Carefully remove from pan and cool completely. Melt remaining 1 tablespoon butter and brush top of cake.

10 to 12 servings.

ALMOND CHOCOLATE TORTE

This torte just may be the ultimate almond and chocolate dessert. A mixture of ground almonds, chocolate, butter, sugar, and eggs is baked to a moist, dense consistency and glazed with more brandy-suffused chocolate.

Torte

1 cup blanched, whole almonds, toasted

9 ounces semisweet chocolate

¼ cup butter

6 eggs, beaten

¾ cup sugar

2 tablespoons flour

¼ cup brandy

Chocolate Glaze

6 tablespoons water

3 tablespoons sugar

3 ounces semisweet chocolate

1 tablespoon brandy

Garnish

Candied violets

In food processor or blender, finely grind almonds; reserve. Generously butter a 9-inch, round cake pan; sprinkle sides and bottom with 2 tablespoons of the ground almonds; reserve. Melt chocolate and butter in double boiler over simmering water. In large bowl, beat eggs with sugar. Beat in chocolate mixture. Beat in flour, remaining ground almonds, and brandy. Pour into prepared pan. Bake at 350° F. for 25 minutes or until toothpick inserted in center comes out almost clean. Cool 10 minutes. Invert torte onto wire rack; remove pan. Cool completely. Meanwhile, prepare Chocolate Glaze. In small saucepan, simmer water and sugar together until sugar dissolves. Add chocolate and brandy. Simmer a few minutes until chocolate melts and glaze coats the back of a spoon. Pour glaze over torte, spreading over top and sides with spatula. If desired, decorate with candied violets.

10 to 12 servings.

APPLE ALMOND TORTE

This is a delicious, buttery apple torte with the distinctive flavor of almond paste. Calvados or apple brandy adds a sophisticated note and intensifies the fruit flavor.

2 medium, green apples, peeled, cored, and sliced ¼-inch thick

½ cup + 1 tablespoon butter, softened, divided

½ cup sugar

6 tablespoons blanched almond paste

2 eggs

¼ teaspoon salt

3 tablespoons Calvados or apple brandy, divided

1 teaspoon vanilla

½ cup cake flour, sifted

4 teaspoons apricot jam

Sauté apples in 1 tablespoon butter over medium heat 2 to 3 minutes or until just tender but not soft; reserve. With fingers work sugar into almond paste until soft and pliable. With electric mixer, add remaining ½ cup butter, making sure no lumps of almond paste remain. Add eggs, one at a time, mixing well after each addition, scraping bowl and beaters frequently. Add salt, 2 tablespoons Calvados, and vanilla. Gradually add flour, beating until smooth. Pour into a buttered and floured 9-inch, round cake pan lined with waxed paper. Arrange apple slices in circular pattern on top. Bake at 350° F. for 45 minutes or until toothpick inserted in center comes out clean. Cool cake in pan; invert and remove waxed paper. Place right side up on plate. Melt jam and remaining 1 tablespoon Calvados in saucepan. Brush mixture on top of torte.

6 to 8 servings.

ALMOND BUTTONS

These sweet little chocolate-laced morsels have a delicate, buttery texture that contrasts perfectly with the crunch of the whole blanched almond. They keep well in the freezer but seem to disappear before they get there.

2 cups blanched, whole almonds, toasted, divided

2 cups flour

¾ cup powdered sugar

¼ teaspoon salt

1 cup + 1½ tablespoons butter, softened, divided

1 teaspoon vanilla

¼ teaspoon almond extract

3 ounces semisweet chocolate

Finely grind 1 cup of the almonds in food processor or blender. Transfer to large bowl. Add flour, sugar, and salt. Thoroughly work in 1 cup butter, vanilla, and almond extract by hand until a soft dough forms. Dough should not crumble. Chill. Shape into ½-inch balls. Place on ungreased cookie sheet; indent center of cookie with finger. Bake at 350° F. for 15 minutes or until done. (Cookies should color only slightly.) Cool. Place chocolate and remaining 1½ tablespoons butter in double boiler; stir over simmering water until smooth. With spoon drizzle *small* amount of chocolate into center of each cookie. Top each with one of the remaining almonds. 8 dozen cookies.

ALMOND COCONUT SQUARES

These chewy, almond and coconut-flavored squares have an appealing moist, brownie-like texture somewhere between a cake and a cookie.

1⅔ cups sliced, natural almonds, toasted, divided

½ cup butter, melted

⅔ cup sugar

1 egg

1½ cups flour

1 cup packed, shredded coconut

1 teaspoon baking powder

¾ cup canned, sweetened coconut cream

Finely grind 1 cup almonds in a food processor or blender; reserve. Combine butter and sugar; stir over medium heat until sugar dissolves. Cool slightly. Beat in egg. Combine flour, coconut, baking powder, and ground almonds; add to butter mixture alternately with coconut cream. Pour into a lightly buttered 13 x 9 x 2-inch baking pan; sprinkle with remaining ⅔ cup sliced almonds, pressing almonds gently into batter. Bake at 350° F. for 25 to 30 minutes or until toothpick inserted in center comes out clean. Cool and cut into squares.

24 squares.

ALMOND SHORTBREAD

Rich, delicate, shortbread dough is laced with crisp, toasted chips of sliced almonds to add new flavor and texture to a popular classic. The very best sweet butter is essential.

1 cup flour

½ cup sifted powdered sugar

¼ cup cornstarch

½ cup butter, softened

¼ teaspoon vanilla extract

¼ teaspoon almond extract

½ cup sliced, natural almonds, toasted and lightly crushed

In food processor, combine flour, sugar, and cornstarch. With short on-off bursts, add butter, extracts, and almonds until mixture just forms a ball. (To prepare shortbread by hand, combine flour, powdered sugar, and cornstarch. With fingertips, work butter into flour mixture until mixture resembles coarse cornmeal. Add extracts and almonds and form dough into ball.) Pat dough into an 8-inch, round pie pan; smooth top of dough. Prick top with fork, and with knife, score into eight wedges. Decorate edge by indenting with tines of a fork. Bake at 350° F. for 25 minutes or until firm.
8 wedges.

FILLED ALMOND CRISPS

This buttery, thin, candy-like nut wafer is rolled into a cylinder and filled with flavored whipped cream. The contrast of the crisp almond cookie with the smooth, velvety filling is a luxurious experience.

⅓ cup + 1 tablespoon butter, divided

½ cup sugar

3 tablespoons flour

2 tablespoons milk

⅛ teaspoon salt

½ cup blanched, slivered almonds, toasted and finely chopped

3 ounces semisweet chocolate

1 recipe of either Orange Liqueur Filling or Strawberry Filling

Orange Liqueur Filling

1½ cups heavy cream

2 tablespoons powdered sugar

2 tablespoons orange liqueur

Diced candied orange peel, for garnish

Strawberry Filling

1½ cups heavy cream

2 teaspoons powdered sugar

¼ teaspoon vanilla

1½ cups whole strawberries, puréed

Combine ⅓ cup butter and next four ingredients; cook and stir over medium heat until smooth. Stir in almonds. Drop by scant tablespoon, about 4 inches apart, onto greased and floured baking sheet. Place only 4 to 6 cookies at one time on a baking sheet. Bake at 350°F. for 5 minutes or until lightly browned. Cool 30 seconds on baking sheet. Carefully lift with wide spatula and place over 1-inch buttered wooden dowel to form tubes; cool. Meanwhile, melt chocolate and remaining 1 tablespoon butter together. Dip each end of wafers into melted chocolate; set on waxed paper to harden. Prepare desired filling. *For Orange Liqueur Filling,* whip cream and powdered sugar until stiff peaks form. Gently fold in orange liqueur. Garnish each end with candied orange peel. *For Strawberry Filling,* whip cream, powdered sugar, and vanilla until stiff peaks form. Gently fold puréed strawberries into whipped cream. Just before serving, with pastry bag, pipe desired filling into cookies.

18 cookies.

144

ALMOND GRAPE TART

Fresh grapes baked in a frangipane filling give this tart a jewel-like appearance and an intense, raisin-sweet flavor. The crisp, almond crust is a perfect textural counterpoint.

Almond Tart Shell

½ cup blanched, whole almonds, toasted

1 cup flour, divided

2 tablespoons sugar

⅛ teaspoon salt

6 tablespoons firm butter

4 to 5 tablespoons cold water

Filling

6 tablespoons sugar

2 egg yolks

⅓ cup heavy cream

¼ cup blanched, whole almonds, toasted, ground

3 cups red or green seedless grapes

To prepare tart shell, finely grind almonds with ½ cup flour in food processor. Add remaining ½ cup flour, sugar, and salt. Add butter and mix with on-off bursts until mixture resembles coarse cornmeal. (To prepare by hand, finely grind almonds with ½ cup flour in blender. Transfer to large bowl. Add remaining ½ cup flour, sugar, and salt. With fingertips, work butter into flour mixture until mixture resembles coarse cornmeal.) Do not overmix. Add enough water to just form dough. Shape dough into ball and chill 30 minutes. Roll dough out on lightly floured board. Fit into a 9-inch tart shell with removable ring and trim edges; chill 30 minutes. Prick bottom of pastry shell with fork. Line with waxed paper, then fill with dried beans. Bake at 400° F. for 10 minutes. Remove paper and beans; reserve shell. To prepare filling, beat together sugar and egg yolks until light yellow. Blend in cream and almonds. Pour into prebaked tart shell. Arrange grapes on filling. Bake at 350° F. for 30 minutes or until top is golden brown.

6 to 8 servings.

ALMOND TART

This tart with French origins quite frankly celebrates almonds. Many popular California restaurants serve a variation of this almond tart. It is easy to make, keeps well, and is simply delicious. Dollops of whipped cream gild the lily nicely. Warning: the baking sheet under the tart pan is essential in case of an overflow.

Tart Shell
1¼ cups flour
1 tablespoon sugar
½ teaspoon salt
6 tablespoons butter
1 egg
Water

Filling
¾ cup heavy cream

¾ cup sugar
1 cup sliced, natural almonds, lightly toasted
2 tablespoons amaretto liqueur (optional)
½ teaspoon vanilla
Pinch salt

To prepare tart shell, combine flour, sugar, and salt. With fingertips, work butter into flour mixture until mixture resembles coarse cornmeal. Do not overmix. Add egg, then drops of water as necessary to just form dough. Shape dough into ball and chill 30 minutes. Roll dough out on lightly floured board. Fit into a 10-inch tart shell with removable ring and trim edges; chill 30 minutes. Prick bottom of pastry shell with fork. Line with waxed paper, then fill with dried beans. Bake at 400° F. for 10 minutes. Remove paper and beans; reserve shell. Stir cream and sugar together over medium heat until sugar dissolves. Stir in almonds, amaretto, vanilla, and salt. Pour into prebaked shell. Place on baking sheet and bake at 350° F. for 30 minutes or until golden brown.

6 to 8 servings.

APPLE TART

In this sophisticated version of an American classic, ground almonds add a delicious, nutty flavor and a crunchy texture to the tart shell, which makes it the perfect complement to the apple filling laced with Calvados. Rich with butter, egg yolks, and nuts, this dessert is best served alone sans any form of cream topping.

Almond Tart Shell

¾ cup blanched, whole almonds, toasted

¾ cup flour, divided

2 tablespoons sugar

⅛ teaspoon salt

6 tablespoons firm butter

4 to 5 tablespoons cold water

Apple Filling

¾ cup sugar

2 tablespoons flour

2 egg yolks

½ cup butter, melted

¼ cup Calvados or apple brandy

2 large apples, peeled, cored, and quartered

To prepare tart shell, finely grind almonds with ½ cup flour in food processor. Add remaining ¼ cup flour, sugar, and salt. Add butter and mix with on-off bursts until mixture resembles coarse cornmeal. (To prepare by hand, finely grind almonds with ½ cup flour in blender. Transfer to large bowl. Add remaining ¼ cup flour, sugar, and salt. With fingertips, work butter into flour mixture until mixture resembles coarse cornmeal.) Do not overmix. Add enough water to just form dough. Shape dough into ball and chill 30 minutes. Roll dough out on lightly floured board. Fit into a 10-inch tart shell with removable ring and trim edges. Prick bottom of pastry shell with fork and chill 30 minutes. Meanwhile, prepare filling. Combine sugar, flour, and egg yolks, beating until smooth. Beat in melted butter. Stir in Calvados; reserve. Cut apple quarters in ⅛-inch slices, keeping pieces together. Arrange each sliced apple quarter in pinwheel pattern in tart shell, fanning slices. Pour filling over apples. Bake at 375° F. for 45 minutes or until filling is lightly browned and crust is golden.

6 to 8 servings.

ALMOND LIME TARTS

Here is a dessert for those who disdain insipid sweetness. The contrast of the rich nuttiness of the almonds and the tart, slightly bitter quality of the lime is refreshing and revives a sated palate.

Tart Shells

½ cup + 2 tablespoons butter, softened

⅓ cup sugar

1 egg, beaten

1¾ cups flour

Lime Curd

2 limes

2 egg yolks

¼ cup sugar

3 tablespoons butter

Almond Filling

1 cup blanched, whole almonds, toasted

1 cup sugar

1 egg

Lime Glaze

1 lime, juiced

½ cup powdered sugar

To prepare tart shells, mix together butter, sugar, and egg until just combined. Add flour all at once and work lightly with fingertips to form dough; do not overmix. Shape dough into a ball and chill 1 hour. Meanwhile, prepare lime curd. Grate peel of both limes and then juice. Combine peel, juice, egg yolks, sugar, and butter in double boiler. Cook, stirring constantly, until thickened, about 3 to 5 minutes; chill. For almond filling, finely grind almonds with sugar in food processor or blender. With machine running, add egg and process just until mixture comes together like a soft dough; reserve. To assemble, roll tart dough out on lightly floured board. Fit in ten, 4-inch tart pans and trim edges. Bake at 400° F. for 5 minutes. Do not brown. Remove from oven and spread bottom of each tart with 2 teaspoons of lime curd. Fill tarts one-half full with almond filling. Smooth tops and bake at 400° F. for 10 to 15 minutes or until lightly browned. Cool completely. Mix lime juice and powdered sugar until smooth, and glaze tops of tarts.

10 tarts.

PEAR AND GINGER TART

Filled with slices of fresh, ripe pear and ginger cream mixture, this tart sings of autumn and winter. Ground almonds add a crisp texture and nutty flavor to the pastry.

Almond Tart Shell

½ cup blanched, slivered almonds, toasted

1 cup flour, divided

2 tablespoons sugar

⅛ teaspoon salt

6 tablespoons firm butter

4 to 5 tablespoons cold water

Pear Filling

½ cup blanched, slivered almonds

1 tablespoon butter

1 egg

½ cup sugar

¼ cup heavy cream

2 tablespoons corn syrup

1 tablespoon finely chopped, crystallized ginger

3 winter pears, peeled

To prepare tart shell, finely grind almonds with ½ cup flour in food processor. Add remaining ½ cup flour, sugar, and salt. Add butter and mix with on-off bursts until mixture resembles coarse cornmeal. (To prepare by hand, finely grind almonds with ½ cup flour in blender. Transfer to large bowl. Add remaining ½ cup flour, sugar, and salt. With fingertips, work butter into flour mixture until mixture resembles coarse cornmeal.) Do not overmix. Add just enough water to form dough. Shape dough into ball and chill 30 minutes. Roll dough out on lightly floured board. Fit into a 9-inch tart shell with removable ring and trim edges; chill 30 minutes. Prick bottom of pastry shell with fork. Line with waxed paper, then fill with dried beans. Bake at 400° F. for 10 minutes. Remove paper and beans; reserve shell. Meanwhile, prepare filling. Sauté almonds in butter until golden; reserve. Beat together egg and sugar. Add cream, corn syrup, and ginger; beat until well-blended. Halve pears lengthwise and remove core with melon baller or teaspoon. Slice and arrange in prebaked tart shell. Pour cream mixture over pears and sprinkle top with almonds. Bake at 325° F. for 45 minutes or until top is lightly browned.

6 to 8 servings.

CHOCOLATE BOURBON PIE

Bourbon, the most American of spirits, perfumes this chocolate-laced dessert that is a delicious cross between a torte and a pie. The nutty crunch of the almond crust pairs perfectly with the moist, chewy texture of the filling.

Almond Pie Shell

½ cup blanched, whole almonds, toasted

1 cup flour, divided

2 tablespoons sugar

⅛ teaspoon salt

6 tablespoons firm butter

4 to 5 tablespoons cold water

Filling

½ cup flour

½ teaspoon baking soda

Pinch salt

½ cup blanched, whole almonds, toasted and ground

¾ cup strong coffee

¼ cup bourbon

2 ounces unsweetened chocolate

½ cup butter

1 cup sugar

1 egg, lightly beaten

½ teaspoon vanilla

Garnish

Whipped cream

To prepare pie shell, finely grind almonds with ½ cup flour in food processor. Add remaining ½ cup flour, sugar, and salt. Add butter and mix with on-off bursts until mixture resembles coarse cornmeal. (To prepare by hand, finely grind almonds with ½ cup flour in blender. Transfer to large bowl. Add remaining ½ cup flour, sugar, and salt. With fingertips, work butter into flour mixture until mixture resembles coarse cornmeal.) Do not overmix. Add just enough water to form dough. Shape dough into ball and chill 30 minutes. Roll out on lightly floured board. Fit into a 9-inch pie pan and trim edges. Prick bottom of pastry shell with fork. Chill 10 minutes. To prepare filling, sift together flour, baking soda, and salt. Stir in almonds; reserve. In a double boiler over simmering water, heat coffee and bourbon. Add chocolate and butter, stirring until smooth and melted. Remove from heat and stir in sugar. Cool 3 minutes. Beat in flour mixture. Add egg and vanilla, beating until smooth. Pour into prepared pie shell. Bake at 275° F. for 1½ hours. Serve with whipped cream.

6 to 8 servings.

BANANAS WITH AMARETTO AND ALMONDS

There is something so elementally wholesome and satisfying about a banana. Perhaps, the soft texture and bland but distinctive sweetness elicits comforting memories of childhood. In this grown-up dessert, the bananas are coated with an amaretto-laced caramel sauce, and their softness is contrasted with the flavorsome crunch of almonds.

⅓ cup butter

¼ cup firmly packed, brown sugar

¼ cup amaretto liqueur

6 bananas, slightly underripe, peeled

⅔ cup blanched, whole almonds, toasted and chopped

In large skillet, melt butter. Add brown sugar and stir until dissolved. Stir in amaretto and ignite by touching the edge of the pan with the flame of a match. Allow to burn until flame dies out. Always use caution when flaming. Place bananas in skillet and cook over medium-high heat, turning occasionally, about 5 minutes or until bananas are heated through and sauce thickens. Stir in almonds. Transfer bananas to serving plate and drizzle sauce over.

6 servings.

NECTARINE GRATIN

Gratins of fresh fruit make marvelous summer desserts. The baking of the fruit allows it to meld with the other ingredients but still retain its individual, fresh quality. In this version, the tart yet sweet taste of nectarines is married with amaretto-spiked cream and topped with a crusty mixture of almonds and brown sugar.

½ cup blanched, whole almonds, toasted
¼ cup firmly packed, brown sugar
2 nectarines
½ cup heavy cream
½ cup sour cream
2 tablespoons amaretto liqueur

Finely grind almonds in food processor or blender with brown sugar; reserve. Slice nectarines and arrange in an 8-inch-square baking dish. Whip heavy cream until barely thickened. Fold in sour cream and amaretto and pour over nectarines. Sprinkle the almond mixture over the dish. Bake at 400° F. for 20 to 30 minutes or until top begins to bubble.

4 to 6 servings.

PEARS WITH GORGONZOLA AND ALMONDS

For those not fond of very sweet things, Pears with Gorgonzola and Almonds is an ideal finish to a meal. The toasted quality and texture of the almonds help to marry the nectar-like ripeness of the pears and the salty bite of the Gorgonzola. This tasty dish is also inviting as a light lunch or a savory snack, with equal aplomb.

1⅓ cups whole, natural almonds, toasted

½ cup butter, softened

6 ounces Gorgonzola cheese

4 ripe pears

Lemon juice

Coarsely grind almonds in food processor or blender; reserve. Combine butter and cheese. Fold in ½ cup almonds; reserve. Peel pears; cut in half lengthwise leaving stem on one side. Scoop out core, seeds, and small amount of flesh with melon baller. Brush with lemon juice to prevent browning. Divide cheese mixture among cavities of four pear halves. Press matching halves on top. Roll pears in remaining almonds. Serve at room temperature.

4 servings.

ALMOND GINGER ICE CREAM

The many small ice cream shops that have sprung up around the country in the last few years have helped stay the decline of America's favorite treat. Today, one can buy high-quality ice cream unadulterated by artificial colors and flavors. Still, there is nothing quite like lifting the paddle out of a homemade mixture, heavy with real cream and real eggs. It is another of life's small pleasures that gives us and our children a sense of process. In this recipe, orange and ginger spark a rich custard mixture shot full of crunchy, buttery almonds.

3 cups heavy cream
1 cup whole milk
¾ cup sugar
2 tablespoons vanilla
4 egg yolks, beaten
6 tablespoons finely chopped, crystallized ginger
1 tablespoon grated orange peel, blanched
1½ cups chopped, natural almonds
2 tablespoons butter

Combine heavy cream, milk, sugar, and vanilla. Cook and stir over medium heat until sugar dissolves and mixture is hot. Gradually add 1 cup of the cream mixture to beaten eggs, whisking constantly. When mixture is smooth, strain into double boiler. Gradually pour in liquid remaining in saucepan, whisking constantly. Cook over simmering water, stirring, until mixture thickens slightly and coats the back of a spoon, about 8 minutes. *Do not boil.* Strain. Stir in crystallized ginger and orange peel; cool. Meanwhile, sauté almonds in butter until crisp; cool. Stir into ice cream mixture. Freeze according to manufacturer's instructions for ice cream freezer.
1 quart.

ESPRESSO PRALINE ICE CREAM

Here's a rich, brandy-infused espresso ice cream that makes a simple but elegant end to a dinner party. Serve in Tulip Cups (page 165) or with crisp cookies.

Praline

¾ cup sugar

1 tablespoon + 2 teaspoons water

1½ cups sliced, natural almonds, toasted

Ice Cream

2 cups heavy cream

2 cups half-and-half

¾ cup sugar

1 tablespoon vanilla extract

1 teaspoon almond extract

5 egg yolks, beaten

2 tablespoons instant espresso powder

2 tablespoons brandy

To prepare praline, mix sugar and water together in a heavy saucepan. Over medium-low heat, cook sugar and water until water evaporates and sugar turns a golden brown, about 5 minutes. Working rapidly, add almonds and stir until all almonds are lightly coated. Spread immediately on a buttered cookie sheet. Cool. Grind coarsely in food processor or crush with a rolling pin until the size of small peas. Reserve. Prepare ice cream by combining heavy cream, half-and-half, sugar, and extracts. Cook and stir over medium heat until sugar dissolves and mixture is hot. Gradually add 1 cup of the cream mixture to beaten egg yolks, whisking constantly. When mixture is smooth, strain into a double boiler. Gradually pour in liquid remaining in saucepan, whisking constantly. Cook over simmering water, stirring, until mixture thickens slightly and coats the back of a spoon, about 8 minutes. *Do not boil.* Combine espresso and brandy in a large bowl. Strain cream mixture into bowl, stirring to dissolve espresso. Cool. Stir in almond praline. Freeze according to manufacturer's instructions for ice cream freezer.

1 quart.

WHITE CHOCOLATE ICE CREAM

White chocolate is a blend of whole milk, sugar, and flavorings condensed to a solid state. Better candy manufacturers add cocoa butter instead of artificial flavors to produce the chocolate flavor and aroma. White chocolate has a sweet, buttery quality with the merest hint of chocolate flavor. In this creamy, almond-studded ice cream, white chocolate combined with the cherry flavor of kirschwasser creates a sumptuous, adult treat.

1 cup whole, natural almonds, coarsely chopped
1 tablespoon butter
3 cups heavy cream
1 cup milk
4 egg yolks
¾ cup sugar
1 tablespoon vanilla extract
½ cup kirschwasser
1 cup grated white chocolate

Sauté almonds in butter until crisp; reserve. Combine cream and milk in a saucepan; cook over medium heat until skin forms. Beat yolks and sugar with vanilla; gradually add cream mixture, whisking constantly. Strain into double boiler and cook over simmering water, stirring, until mixture thickens and lightly coats the back of a spoon, about 10 minutes. *Do not boil.* Remove from heat and add kirschwasser and white chocolate, stirring until chocolate melts. Cool to room temperature. Add almonds and freeze according to manufacturer's instructions for ice cream freezer.
1 quart.

ALMOND AMARETTO PARFAIT

Praline, a mixture of almonds and caramelized sugar, is a useful confection to have on hand. Sprinkle it on ice cream or add it to cookies, cakes, and candy. Here it adds crunch and flavor to a creamy, amaretto-laced mousse.

Praline

½ cup sugar

1 tablespoon water

1 cup sliced, natural almonds, toasted

Mousse Mixture

1 envelope or 2½ teaspoons unflavored gelatin

½ cup sugar

4 eggs, separated

1½ cups milk

½ cup amaretto liqueur

Pinch salt

1½ cups heavy cream

Garnish

Whipped cream

Sliced, natural almonds, toasted

To prepare praline, mix sugar and water together in a heavy saucepan. Over medium-low heat, cook sugar and water until water evaporates and sugar turns a golden brown, about 5 minutes. Working rapidly, add almonds and stir until all almonds are lightly coated. Spread immediately on a buttered cookie sheet. Cool. Grind coarsely in food processor or crush with a rolling pin until the size of small peas. Reserve. Mix gelatin and sugar in saucepan. Beat egg yolks and milk together and add to gelatin mixture. Cook over low heat, stirring constantly, until gelatin is dissolved, about 5 minutes. *Do not boil.* Stir in amaretto. Pour into large bowl and chill, stirring occasionally, until mixture mounds slightly when dropped from a spoon, about 1 hour. Stir in praline mixture. Beat egg whites and salt until stiff but not dry. Fold thoroughly into gelatin mixture. Beat cream until soft peaks form. Fold thoroughly into egg-white mixture. Divide among eight, 8-ounce parfait glasses. Chill at least 3 hours. Decorate with whipped cream and toasted almonds.
8 servings.

Variation:
For Almond Lemon Parfait, increase sugar in mousse mixture to ¾ cup and substitute the juice of one whole lemon and the grated peel of ½ lemon for the amaretto.

Soufflés continue to hold magic for the most jaded of palates. The light, airy texture and delicate but definite flavor are a perfect way to end a festive dinner. Here, the distinctive taste of almond paste in the soufflé is contrasted with a tart, fruity sauce of raspberry purée.

Soufflé

¼ cup + 2 tablespoons sugar, divided

1 cup blanched almond paste

1½ cups milk, divided

3 tablespoons butter

3 tablespoons flour

¼ teaspoon salt

6 eggs, separated, plus 1 additional egg white

2 tablespoons orange liqueur

¼ teaspoon cream of tartar

Raspberry Sauce

1 quart fresh raspberries or 2 packages, 10 ounces each, frozen raspberries

Sugar

Generously butter a 2½-quart soufflé dish; sprinkle with 1 tablespoon sugar and reserve. Knead almond paste with fingers until soft and pliable. In food processor or blender, combine almond paste and ½ cup milk until smooth; reserve. Melt butter and stir in flour. Blend in remaining 1 cup milk; cook, stirring constantly, until thickened. Add ¼ cup sugar, salt, and almond-paste mixture; heat through. Remove from heat and beat in egg yolks, one at a time. Stir in orange liqueur. Beat egg whites with remaining 1 tablespoon sugar and cream of tartar until stiff but not dry. Mix one-fourth egg-white mixture thoroughly into almond-paste mixture. Gently fold in remaining egg-white mixture. Pour into prepared soufflé dish. Bake at 350° F. for 30 to 35 minutes. Meanwhile, purée raspberries and strain through fine sieve. Add sugar to taste. To serve, pour small amount of Raspberry Sauce on each plate and top with portion of soufflé.

8 to 10 servings.

ALMOND CREME BRULEE

Traditionally, Crème Brûlée is a rich mixture of heavy cream and egg yolks topped by a crust of brown sugar. The contrast of the crisp bits of caramelized sugar and the silky, thick cream mixture is a sensual delight. In this version, the flavor and texture of almonds add a deliciously new element.

6 egg yolks

½ cup sugar

2 cups heavy cream, heated

¼ teaspoon almond extract

¾ cup whole, natural almonds, toasted, and coarsely ground, divided

¼ cup firmly packed, dark brown sugar

Beat egg yolks and sugar until slightly thickened. Slowly beat in hot cream. Add almond extract and ½ cup almonds. Pour into individual custard or soufflé dishes. Place in roasting pan and add enough water to pan to come halfway up sides of dishes. Bake at 250° F. for 2 hours or until custard is set. Remove from roasting pan and let cool. Combine remaining ¼ cup almonds and brown sugar and divide among custard dishes, packing tops. Mist with water. (A plant mister works well here.) Glaze under broiler until sugar melts.

6 servings.

AMARETTO CHEESECAKE

*The subject of cheesecake, like choco-
late, generates heated discussions
and unyielding opinions. The one
thing all agree upon is that
real cheesecake must be baked—no
shortcut chilled-gelatin mixtures
here. Amaretto Cheesecake is a sub-
stantial version, dense with
ricotta yet balanced by a good
quantity of cream cheese. The
amaretto cookies and liqueur per-
fume all, and the texture of
chopped almond relieves the smooth
richness of the cheeses.*

2 tablespoons butter, melted, divided

4 amaretto cookies (¼ cup graham-
cracker crumbs may be substituted)

1 cup blanched, whole almonds,
toasted, divided

8 ounces ricotta cheese

1½ pounds cream cheese

5 eggs

1 cup sugar

¼ cup amaretto liqueur

1 teaspoon almond extract

Brush bottom of 10-inch springform pan with 1 tablespoon melted butter. Finely grind cookies, ½ cup almonds, and remaining 1 tablespoon melted butter in food processor or blender. Sprinkle evenly over bottom of pan and press down. Beat ricotta until smooth. Gradually beat in cream cheese until well-blended. Add eggs, one at a time, alternating with sugar and ending with last egg. Scrape down sides of bowl to insure even mixing and smooth texture. Finely chop remaining ½ cup almonds and add to cream-cheese mixture along with amaretto and almond extract. Pour into prepared pan. Bake at 350° F. for 15 minutes. Reduce heat to 200° F. and continue baking 1 hour longer. Do not open oven door during first 30 minutes of baking time. Turn off heat and allow cheesecake to cool in oven 2 hours. Remove cheesecake and transfer to serving dish.

8 to 10 servings.

SARONNO FUDGE

Chopped almonds and amaretto liqueur make this creamy, intensely flavored fudge the perfect gift for almond lovers.

4 cups sugar

2 cups heavy cream

¼ teaspoon salt

¾ cup amaretto liqueur, divided

1½ cups chopped, natural almonds

2 tablespoons butter

In large saucepan, combine sugar, cream, salt, and ½ cup amaretto. Cook and stir over medium heat until sugar is dissolved. Bring to a boil and cook, without stirring, until mixture reaches 234° F. (soft-ball stage). Remove from heat and without stirring cool to 110° F. While mixture is cooling, sauté almonds in butter until crisp. Reserve. When fudge is cool, add remaining ¼ cup amaretto and almonds. Beat until creamy, about 3 minutes, and pour into a buttered, 8-inch-square pan. Let set until firm and cut into squares.

25 squares.

TULIP CUPS

These cunning little crisp, almond-flavored cups are perfect for serving fresh fruit sorbets or building sinful ice cream desserts. Very useful to keep on hand for sweet emergencies. Store in an air-tight container.

½ cup blanched almond paste

6 tablespoons sugar

2 egg whites

5 tablespoons flour

⅔ cup heavy cream

1 tablespoon kirschwasser

Knead almond paste with fingers until soft and pliable. Combine softened almond paste and sugar. Beat in egg whites, one at a time, then flour. Add cream and kirschwasser, beating until smooth, about 3 to 5 minutes. Turn a cookie sheet upside down; grease and lightly flour bottom. Put 1 generous tablespoon batter on pan, using spatula or bottom of the tablespoon to spread batter out into a flat, thin circle, 5 to 6 inches in diameter. If batter seems too thick, thin with an extra tablespoon of cream. Bake at 350° F. for 8 to 10 minutes or until lightly browned. Let rest 30 seconds on cookie sheet. While still hot, remove from cookie sheet and place over upside-down small bowl, about 3 inches in diameter. Place second small bowl over the cookie to press down and form cup shape. If cookies become too cool to form, place back in oven for 1 minute to soften.

About 15 tulip cups.

FRESH CHEESE WITH CHARTREUSE

Here is a creamy, sweet cheese spread with a hint of green Chartreuse. It needs the contrast of delicate, faintly salty crackers—like those crisp, white discs imported from England. Fresh Cheese with Chartreuse makes a marvelous combination cheese and dessert course.

½ cup chopped, natural almonds

3 tablespoons butter, softened, divided

8 ounces cream cheese

2 tablespoons green Chartreuse liqueur

3 tablespoons powdered sugar

Sauté almonds in 1 tablespoon butter until crisp; reserve. Combine cheese, remaining 2 tablespoons butter, and Chartreuse. Beat in powdered sugar. Fold in almonds. 4 servings.

ALMOND FRENCH TOAST

6 eggs, lightly beaten
¾ cup heavy cream
6 tablespoons melted butter
1 tablespoon sugar

¼ teaspoon freshly grated nutmeg
12 slices bread
¾ cup chopped, natural almonds, toasted

When bread is no longer quite soft enough for sandwiches, it is perfect for French toast. A leisurely soak in a rich blend of eggs, cream, and butter makes a lovely, custardy version of this classic. Almond French Toast bakes in a hot oven, which allows the cook easily to have a number of servings ready all at once. It is as good for Sunday-night supper as it is for breakfast. A light dusting of powdered sugar — or maple syrup for the hard-core — is all that is needed.

Beat together eggs, cream, melted butter, sugar, and nutmeg. Soak bread in egg mixture, turning once. Place bread on a well-buttered cookie sheet. (May be prepared ahead to this point and refrigerated.) Bake bread at 400° F. for about 5 minutes until underside is golden brown. Turn and top each slice with 1 tablespoon almonds. Bake about 6 minutes longer until underside is golden brown.

6 servings.

ALMOND SWISS BAKED EGGS

These eggs are delicious and easy to prepare. Double or triple the recipe, if you like, but bake a bit longer to compensate. Almond Swiss Baked Eggs *can be assembled in advance up to the final addition of almonds and melted butter and held in the refrigerator, although the cooking time will also be extended.*

½ cup heavy cream

¼ cup dry white wine

¼ teaspoon freshly grated nutmeg

8 tablespoons grated Swiss cheese, divided

4 tablespoons finely chopped onion, divided

8 eggs, divided

½ cup sliced, natural almonds, toasted, divided

6 teaspoons melted butter, divided

Mix cream, wine, and nutmeg; reserve. Butter 4 gratin dishes. Sprinkle each dish with 2 tablespoons cheese and 1 tablespoon onion. Crack 2 eggs into each dish. Pour 3 tablespoons of cream mixture over eggs. Sprinkle with 2 tablespoons almonds. Drizzle 1½ teaspoons melted butter over almonds. Bake at 350° F. for 8 to 10 minutes or until done. Yolks should be soft and whites just set.

4 servings.

MARMALADE BREAD

With good reason, Marmalade Bread suggests visions of hot tea and a cozy fire. It is also delicious sliced thinly and toasted for breakfast. The ingredients are never out of season and can be purchased readily. Use as good a quality marmalade as the budget will allow.

¾ cup chopped, natural almonds

⅓ cup + 1 tablespoon butter, softened, divided

2 cups flour

1 tablespoon baking powder

½ teaspoon salt

½ cup sugar

1 egg

½ cup orange marmalade

½ cup orange juice

½ cup Scotch whisky

Sauté almonds in 1 tablespoon butter until crisp; reserve. Sift together flour, baking powder, and salt; reserve. Cream remaining ⅓ cup butter and sugar until fluffy. Beat in egg, then marmalade, then orange juice and Scotch. Continue beating on low speed, gradually adding the flour mixture. Fold in almonds. Pour into a greased and floured 9 x 5 x 3-inch loaf pan and bake at 325° F. for 1 hour or until toothpick inserted in center comes out clean.

1 loaf.

ALMOND CARDAMOM BREAD

This quick bread has the intriguing flavor of cardamom softened by hints of orange. By all means use whole cardamom seeds if possible—the flavor is far superior to the ground spice. Toast thin slices for breakfast or serve it at tea with butter that has been spiked with grated orange peel.

3 cups flour

⅔ cup sugar

4 teaspoons baking powder

½ teaspoon salt

¼ teaspoon cardamom seeds, crushed

1¼ cups milk

1 egg

¼ cup orange juice

1 tablespoon grated orange peel

3 tablespoons melted butter

¾ cup chopped, natural almonds, toasted

Combine first five ingredients; reserve. Combine milk, egg, orange juice, and peel. Stir milk mixture into dry ingredients. Stir in butter. Add almonds. Pour into a greased and floured 9 x 5-inch loaf pan. Bake at 350° F. for 1 hour or until toothpick inserted in center comes out clean.

1 loaf.

GINGER LEMON BREAD

There is something so elementally satisfying about making yeast breads —that direct and physical link between labor and reward that is so often missing in our contemporary world. Ginger Lemon Bread is an especial opportunity, because extra kneading effort is called for to incorporate the bits of lemon, ginger, and almonds. A relaxed baker and four round, aromatic loaves are the just rewards.

3 cups chopped, natural almonds

½ cup + 3 tablespoons butter, softened, divided

½ cup + 1 tablespoon sugar

2 packages, ¼ ounce each, active dry yeast

2 cups warm (110° F.) milk, divided

2½ tablespoons honey

2 teaspoons vanilla

6 cups flour

1 teaspoon salt

1 lemon, including peel, finely diced

1 cup finely chopped, crystallized ginger

1 egg, beaten with 2 teaspoons water

Sauté almonds in 3 tablespoons butter and 1 tablespoon sugar until crisp; reserve. Dissolve yeast in 1 cup milk mixed with the honey and vanilla; let rest 10 minutes. Combine flour, salt, and remaining ½ cup sugar; add yeast mixture. Add remaining 1 cup milk; mix dough to form ball. Cut remaining ½ cup butter into small pieces and knead into dough, until all butter has been absorbed. Continue kneading 15 minutes or until dough is smooth and elastic. Form into ball, place in buttered mixing bowl, and cover with plastic wrap. Let rise in warm place 2 hours or until doubled in volume. Punch dough down. Sprinkle lemon, ginger, and almonds on dough; knead on floured board until all ingredients are incorporated thoroughly. Divide dough and shape into 4 round loaves. Cover with damp cloth and let rise 45 minutes or until doubled in volume. Brush with beaten egg and water. Bake loaves on 2 baking sheets at 350° F. for 35 to 45 minutes or until golden brown. 4 loaves.

ALMOND CINNAMON FOCACCIA

Focaccia is made from a dense, yeasty dough aromatic with good, fruity olive oil. It is first cousin to pizza, baked flat, with only a hint of topping. Herb, tomato, garlic or onion are some of the flavors of the savory variety. Here is a sweet version—especially suited for breakfast or brunch—or anytime a serious snack is required.

2 packages, ¼ ounce each, active dry yeast
1½ cups warm (110° F.) water
2 cups flour
1½ cups cake flour
1 cup sugar, divided
½ teaspoon salt

½ cup + 3 tablespoons olive oil, divided
1 tablespoon cinnamon
¼ cup butter, melted
1 cup sliced, natural almonds, toasted

Dissolve yeast in water. Combine flours, ½ cup sugar, and salt; stir into yeast mixture. Gradually add ½ cup oil, stirring constantly, mixing just to form dough. Cover and let rise in a warm place until doubled in volume, about 1½ hours. Combine remaining ½ cup sugar and cinnamon; reserve. Grease a 17 x 11-inch pan with remaining 3 tablespoons oil; spread dough into pan. Brush top with melted butter; sprinkle with toasted almonds, pressing almonds firmly into dough. Sprinkle with cinnamon-sugar mixture. Let rise in a warm place, 15 to 20 minutes. Bake at 375° F. for 20 to 25 minutes. Cut into squares.

20 squares.

SPICED ALMONDS

This is the yummy kind of nut confection that even people who don't care for sweets can't seem to stop munching. An excellent gift!

1 cup sugar

6 tablespoons milk

½ teaspoon cinnamon

½ teaspoon cream of tartar

¼ teaspoon salt

½ teaspoon vanilla

2 cups whole, natural almonds, toasted

Combine first five ingredients. Cook, without stirring, to soft-ball stage (234° F.). Remove from heat and stir in vanilla and almonds. Turn onto waxed paper and quickly separate almonds with a fork. Cool.

2 cups.

CRYSTALLIZED ALMONDS

The perfect balance between salt and sugar in these nibbling almonds is a delight and excitement to the palate. They are awfully good with a preprandial glass of champagne or sherry, but then, they are just awfully good.

1 teaspoon vegetable oil

1 cup blanched, whole almonds, lightly toasted

½ teaspoon salt

2 tablespoons sugar

Heat oil in small skillet. Add almonds and toss until coated with oil. Add salt, stirring constantly. Over medium heat, gradually add sugar, stirring constantly. When almonds are golden and all sugar is dissolved, remove from pan and let cool.
1 cup.

BELGIAN ENDIVE WITH GORGONZOLA AND ALMONDS

Belgian endive is becoming available more readily during most of the year, but it is still pricey. This recipe stretches three endives into canapés for a group and takes advantage of the distinctive shape of the spears. Other creamy, soft cheeses can be substituted for the Gorgonzola, or all cream cheese can be used.

½ cup chopped, natural almonds
1 tablespoon butter
4 tablespoons Gorgonzola cheese
3½ ounces cream cheese
1 tablespoon brandy
½ tablespoon lemon juice
Pinch cayenne
30 leaves Belgian endive, approximately 3 endives

Sauté almonds in butter until crisp; reserve. Combine Gorgonzola, cream cheese, brandy, lemon juice, and cayenne in food processor until blended, or mix together by hand. Place a small teaspoon of cheese mixture on base of each endive leaf. Lightly press cheese into almonds.

30 canapés.

FRESH CHEESE WITH HERBS

M.F.K. Fisher wrote a wonderful essay on the matter of dips. She does not suffer dips. However, she is willing to consider, both intellectually and gastronomically, spreads. She once took one to a neighborhood gathering. This cheese mixture is quite certainly a spread, full of almonds, and fresh herbs, kissed with good olive oil. It tops a bagel or melba toast with equal aplomb.

⅔ cup chopped, natural almonds
3 tablespoons olive oil, divided
1 pound cream cheese, softened
¼ cup heavy cream
2 teaspoons red wine vinegar
2 cloves garlic, chopped finely

2 tablespoons chopped, fresh parsley
3 tablespoons chopped, fresh chives
  or 1 tablespoon dried chives
1 tablespoon chopped, fresh tarragon
  or 1 teaspoon dried tarragon
½ teaspoon salt

Sauté almonds in 1 tablespoon oil until crisp. Cool. Meanwhile, combine cream cheese and heavy cream. Add remaining 2 tablespoons oil and the vinegar. Fold in remaining ingredients and the almonds. Chill 3 hours.
Makes 3½ cups.

SWEET BRIE

This recipe may well make the purist shudder, but the rich flavor of the Brie is perfectly punctuated by the almonds, whisky, and brown sugar glaze. The brief baking enhances the sumptuousness of the cheese.

1 cup firmly packed, golden brown sugar

¾ cup chopped, natural almonds, toasted

2 tablespoons Scotch whisky

1 tablespoon honey

1 8-inch-round Brie, about 2 pounds

Combine brown sugar, almonds, Scotch, and honey. Place Brie on a shallow, ovenproof serving dish. Cover top with almond mixture. Bake at 550° F. for 4 to 8 minutes until sugar bubbles and melts, and Brie warms through.

ON ALMONDS

Selection Unshelled almonds should be clean and free from scars, cracks or holes; the kernels should not rattle. Shelled almonds should be plump, meaty, and crisp. A limp or shriveled nut is stale.

Forms <u>Whole Natural</u> – shelled almonds still wearing their brown skins.
<u>Sliced Natural</u> – whole, brown-skinned almonds that have been sliced thinly lengthwise.
<u>Chopped Natural</u> – whole, brown-skinned almonds that have been coarsely chopped.
<u>Blanched Whole</u> – shelled almonds with their brown skins removed. (To blanch whole natural almonds, cover almonds with boiling water. Let stand 3 minutes and then test to see if skins slip off easily. Remove almonds from water one at a time, slip off skins and let dry on paper towel several hours.)
<u>Blanched Slivered</u> – blanched almonds that have been split into halves, then cut lengthwise in long, narrow pieces.

Volumes and Measures 1 cup sliced almonds = 3¼ ounces
1 cup slivered almonds = 4½ ounces
1 cup whole almonds (shelled) = 5 ounces
1 cup (5 ounces) whole almonds will yield approximately 1¼ cups when ground in blender or food processor.

Storage Store almonds in tightly sealed containers, in a cool dry place such as the refrigerator. Stored this way, almonds and almond paste will stay fresh for months. Almonds kept in the freezer will stay fresh even longer.

Toasting   Spread almonds in a single layer in a shallow pan. Bake blanched whole almonds, stirring often, at 300° F. for 15 minutes or until they just begin to turn color. Bake whole natural almonds, stirring often, at 300° F. for 15 minutes or until almonds are crisp and toasted in flavor. After removing almonds from the oven, they will continue to toast slightly due to the heat retained in each nut. Time is approximate. Smaller quantities and smaller almond pieces will toast faster.

Nutrition Information

Serving Size	1 ounce (about 20-25 nuts)
Calories	170
Protein	6 grams
Carbohydrates	5 grams
Fat	14 grams
Polyunsaturated	3 grams
Saturated	1 gram
Cholesterol	0
Sodium	4 mg.

Almonds provide significant amounts of essential vitamins and minerals, such as Vitamin E, riboflavin, magnesium, and phosphorus. No cholesterol is the added bonus.

(Nutrition information supplied by the Almond Board of California, Sacramento, California.)

Almond Butter   To prepare ½ cup of almond butter, grind 1 cup toasted blanched whole almonds in food processor or blender until coarse in texture. With machine running, add ½ tablespoon vegetable oil and continue to process until texture is smooth. This recipe can be easily doubled or tripled when a larger quantity of almond butter is desired.

amontillado	a designation for sherry that is moderately sweet with a fairly dry finish. True sherry comes from Spain but acceptable substitutes are produced in this country.
baguette	a long, slender loaf of French bread, generally about 3 to 3½ inches in diameter.
balsamic vinegar	an aged Italian vinegar made from a sweet wine. Aceto Balsamico is dark brown in color, intense in flavor, and quite acidic. A good red wine vinegar may be substituted, although the character of the finished dish will be altered.
Belgian endive	a member of the chicory family that grows in tight heads of pale spears. The texture is crisp and the flavor is slightly bitter. Peak season is from late summer through winter. Although expensive, there is little waste.
fresh white bread crumbs	fresh white bread crumbs are superior in texture to commercially prepared bread crumbs. Trim the crusts of day-old French bread or other coarse-textured bread and discard. Whirl bread in blender until finely ground.
Brie	a creamy French cheese with a delicate, nutty flavor. Brie is available in various sized rounds from cheese and specialty stores.
butter	the quality of the butter depends on the cream from which it is made. Sweet butter is preferred in these recipes. Salted butter often masks unpleasant or off flavors in the butter and allows the cook less control over the amount of salt added.
Calvados	an apple brandy from the Normandy region of France. Domestic apple brandy or apple jack may be substituted.

caramelized sugar	sugar that has been cooked slowly, usually with a small amount of water, until it melts and reaches a golden color and syrupy consistency.
cellophane noodles	noodles made from powdered mung beans. They appear brittle and whitish colored until soaked, when they become transparent and supple. Vermicelli pasta may be substituted.
Chartreuse	an aromatic, herbaceous French liqueur available in two forms: green, which has a high alcoholic strength, and yellow, which is sweeter and not so potent.
chicken stock	fresh, homemade chicken stock is far superior in flavor to commercially manu-factured stock. If canned stock is used as a substitute, reduce the amount of salt in the recipe to compensate for the excessive salt in most canned stocks.
cilantro	also known as Mexican parsley or Chinese parsley, it is actually the leaf of the coriander plant. It has a zesty, pungent flavor.
coarse salt	the form of salt used with old-fashioned ice cream freezers. It is often sold as Rock Salt.
coconut cream	a rich syrup made from sugar and coconut purée. It is used as an ingredient for making tropical drinks.
cream cheese	a slightly tangy and soft, fresh cheese. Most specialty cheese stores sell a variety made without additives that is superior in flavor and texture to the pre-packaged varieties.

crème fraîche	a thick cream fermented by lacto-bacteria to produce a rich, slightly sour cream used commonly in France. You may make a reasonable facsimile by stirring 1 teaspoon buttermilk into 1 cup heavy cream and carefully heating to lukewarm, 85° F. Allow to stand at room temperature until it has thickened (approximately 24 hours). Stir and refrigerate.
crushed	spices and seeds may be crushed with a mortar and pestle or by placing between 2 pieces of waxed paper and smashing with the bottom of a heavy saucepan.
crystallized or candied ginger	sliced ginger that has been preserved with sugar.
deglaze	to deglaze, add the specified liquid and stir over heat until the pan drippings are dissolved into the liquid.
degrease	tilt the pan and use a large spoon to skim off the fat that rises to the surface.
flour	a blend of hard and soft wheat flours, bleached or unbleached all-purpose flour should be used unless another type of flour is specified in recipe.
goat cheese	called *Chèvres* in France, these cheeses are tangy when young and more intense in flavor as they age. Domestic goat cheese is now available in many areas.
Gorgonzola	a creamy Italian blue cheese that is pungent and salty. Other varieties of blue cheese may be substituted, although the character of the finished dish will be altered.

182

gratin	this term refers to a sauced dish with a topping of bread crumbs or finely ground nuts, which is then browned in the oven or under the broiler. It is usually served in the dish it's baked in.
gratin dish	a shallow, ovenproof dish used for baking and serving.
hoisin sauce	a dark, sweet paste made from vinegar, sugar, chile powder, sesame, and fermented wheat or soybeans. Often available in the gourmet or Chinese section at larger supermarkets, hoisin sauce may be kept indefinitely in a covered container in the refrigerator.
jalapeño pepper	a small, green hot pepper that is available fresh or canned. Removing the seeds will make it less hot.
julienne	vegetables or other foods cut into small strips the size of matchsticks.
kirschwasser	a distilled spirit made from cherries. Also known as Kirsch, most is imported from Germany; however, less expensive, domestic brands are available.
mussels	available year-round through many seafood purveyors, mussels range in color from pale tan to brilliant orange. Buy them from a reliable fishmonger with a high turnover. Clean shells thoroughly and use only those that open when cooked.
nutmeg	the hard inner kernel of *myristica frangrans*. For best flavor, grind only as much as is needed at a time in a nutmeg grinder or use a small grater.
olive oil	the fresh fruit of the olive tree is crushed in a press to produce a distinctively

183

flavored oil that tastes of the olive. Virgin olive oil is cold-pressed and without additives. It varies from sweet and pale gold to pungent and greenish gold. Extra-virgin is the first and superior pressing. Second pressing oils, labeled virgin, fine, or extra-fine are not as delicately flavored but adequate for recipes in which the flavor of other ingredients predominate. Olive oils labeled "pure" are inferior third pressings in which heat and chemicals have been used to extract the oil.

Parmesan an extremely hard Italian cheese with a complex, sharp, salty flavor. Whole Parmesan cheese is available at many delicatessens or specialty cheese stores and is sold by the piece or wedge. Grate only as much as you need at one time, then wrap the remainder in plastic and store in the freezer. Freshly grated Parmesan cheese is far superior to pre-grated, dried cheese.

poaching moist heat cooking with a liquid that is barely simmering or "shivering" as the French say. A lid or parchment paper cover is used to create steam for self-basting.

purée to change a solid food into a thick paste. This can be done most conveniently in a blender or a food processor.

reduce to simmer or boil a sauce or stock, evaporating water, until it is thicker and more intense in flavor.

rice vinegar a sweet, mild vinegar produced in both Chinese and Japanese styles. The Japanese vinegar is more readily available.

sear to brown meat quickly over a high heat, sealing the surface to prevent loss of juices and sticking.

shallots	a cross between garlic and onion. Shallots are used when a subtle, mild onion flavor is desired. The white portion of the green onion may be substituted. Store in a cool, dry place. Do not refrigerate.
snails	also called *escargot*, are small gastropods. Usually imported from France and packed 12 to a can, they are available in grocery stores or specialty food shops.
soft ball stage (234° F-240° F)	when a few drops of syrup dropped into a cup of ice water can be formed into a ball that flattens and loses its shape when taken out of the water.
soy sauce	although the manufacturing process is much the same, Japanese soy sauce and Chinese soy sauce are quite different in flavor. Japanese soy sauce is much sweeter and less salty than its Chinese counterpart. When shopping for soy sauce, buy one without additives such as corn syrup or caramel.
spiced green olives	large, green olives preserved in brine flavored with garlic, chile pepper and other spices.
springform pan	a baking pan with a removable rim. Available in various sizes, the springform pan is traditionally used for cheesecakes and other heavy cakes.
tomato	properly ripened, fresh red tomatoes are an important ingredient in good cooking. Fresh tomatoes should be ripened at room temperature away from direct sunlight. Tomatoes stored at cold temperatures (below 55° F.) never reach optimum flavor and texture. If fresh tomatoes are unavailable, canned Italian plum tomatoes make a good substitution.

185

sweet Brie, 177

cheese, blue:
  Belgian endive with Gorgonzola and
    almonds, 175
  and celery salad, 36
  fettuccine Gorgonzola, 20
  pears with almonds and Gorgonzola,
    156

cheese, goat:
  chicken breasts stuffed with, 78
  chicken ragout with chiles, tortil-
    las, and, 83
  mushrooms stuffed with, 8
  papaya, and watercress salad, 29

cheesecake, amaretto, 163

chicken, 77-96
  almond Dijon, 82
  almond, paprika, 81
  almond, with onion, 88
  baked, with almonds, mushrooms, and
    olives, 90
  baked curried, 84
  with brandy and cream, 89
  California, mole, 87
  cornbread and sausage stuffed, 85
  lemon marmalade, 95
  livers and almonds Madeira, 94
  with plums, 93
  ragout with chiles, tortillas, and
    goat cheese, 83
  and rice with black olives, fennel,
    and orange, 91
  roast, with honey, black pepper, and

almonds, 86
  and roasted peppers, 92

chicken breast, 77-80
  with almonds and green grapes, 77
  with orange and mustard, 80
  sautéed with coriander and orange,
    79
  stuffed with goat cheese, 78

chicken salad:
  Chinese-style almond, 45
  Mexican-style almond, 44

Chinese-style:
  almond chicken salad, 45
  almond pasta, 42

chives:
  artichoke sauté with mustard and, 76
  zucchini with orange and, 57

chocolate:
  almond cake, 133
  almond torte, 139
  bourbon pie, 153
  California chicken mole, 87
  white, ice cream, 159

cinnamon almond focaccia, 172

coconut:
  almond rice, 61
  almond squares, 142
  pork ragout with curry and, 111

cod:
  filet of, with garlic mayonnaise and
    green chiles, 128

rock, with jalapeño salsa, 127

cookies, 141-45
  almond buttons, 141
  almond coconut squares, 142
  almond shortbread, 143
  filled almond crisps, 144

coriander, chicken breasts sautéed
  with orange and, 79

cornbread and sausage stuffed
  chicken, 85

crab salad with Belgian endive and
  kiwi fruit, 46

cream:
  chicken with brandy and, 89
  vermouth sauce, sole with, 122

crème brûlée, almond, 162

crystallized almonds, 174

cumin:
  honey pork with rice, 112
  shrimp with lime and, 115

curried, curry:
  almond apple soup, 1
  almond tuna salad, 51
  baked chicken, 84
  egg salad, 4
  lamb apricot, 109
  pork ragout with coconut and, 111
  scallops and spinach fettuccine with
    sauce of, 21

lemon bread, 171
-lime butter, almond sole with, 123
melon with basil and, 3
and pear tart, 152
vinaigrette, shrimp and noodles
with, 22

Gorgonzola:
Belgian endive with almonds and, 175
fettuccine, 20
pears with almonds and, 156

grape:
almond tart, 147
green, chicken breasts with almonds
and, 77
and watercress salad, 31

H

halibut, baked filets of, with tomatoed béarnaise sauce, 126

herbs:
cheese tart, 11
fresh cheese with, 176
potatoes with cheese and, 63

honey:
cumin pork with rice, 112
roast chicken with black pepper,
almonds, and, 86

I

ice cream, 157-59
almond ginger, 157
espresso praline, 158

white chocolate, 159

Italian sausage:
and cornbread stuffed chicken, 85
and rice, 113

K

kiwi, crab salad with Belgian
endive and, 46

L

lamb, 105-9
apricot curry, 109
chops with almond-Parmesan cheese
coating, 105
meatballs, 23
rack of, with almond Madeira sauce,
107-8

leek, creamed, and toast points, 13

lemon:
almond pound cake, 132
ginger bread, 171
marmalade chicken, 95
warm steak salad with pepper and, 50

lime:
almond tarts, 150
figs with pepper and, 2
-ginger butter, almond sole with,
123
shrimp with cumin and, 115

liver, chicken, and almonds
Madeira, 94

M

Madeira:
almond sauce, rack of lamb with,
107-8
chicken livers and almonds, 94

marmalade:
bread, 169
lemon, chicken, 95

mayonnaise, garlic, filet of cod with
green chiles and, 128

meat, *see* beef; lamb; pork; veal

meatballs, lamb, 23

melon with basil and ginger, 3

Mexican-style almond chicken
salad, 44

mint:
pasta with mustard and, 17
pilaf, 60

mousse, almond amaretto parfait,
160

mushroom:
baked chicken with almonds, olives,
and, 90
broiled, 65
scallops with Scotch whisky and, 120
stuffed with goat cheese, 8

mussels, baked, with almonds and
Pernod, 25

vinaigrette:
  almond, grilled steak with, 101
  ginger, shrimp and noodles with, 22
  mustard, vegetable mélange mari-
    nated in, 39
  pepper, red bell, salmon filets
    with, 130

volumes and measures, 178

W

watercress:
  and apple salad, 30
  goat cheese, and papaya salad, 29
  and grape salad, 31

Z

zucchini:
  almond fried, 58
  with orange and chives, 57
  sautéed, 59
  summer squash mock pasta, 54

Notes

Notes

Notes

Notes

Notes